PSYCHOLOGICAL RESEARCH AND

HUMAN VALUES

PSYCHOLOGICAL RESEARCH AND HUMAN VALUES

By

LUCIEN A. BUCK

Professor of Psychology
Dowling College

THE CHRISTOPHER PUBLISHING HOUSE
NORTH QUINCY, MASSACHUSETTS 02171

To Beverly

INTRODUCTION

Generally, psychological researchers have behaved as if the scientific enterprise was value-free. At a time when technology is being questioned both from outside and within the scientific community, psychologists must confront the value structure implicit in their traditional research strategies. It is necessary to begin a critical assessment of the particular model of Man promoted by "scientific" criteria such as "objectivity," "control" and "environmentalism" and by the type of research method selected—"experimentalism."

Psychologists have a choice, and the consequences of these decisions are crucial to the future of society. Szasz (1970, pp. 190-217) has elaborately described the dehumanizing, demeaning outcome of the "scientific" classification of mental illness. Psychiatric classification is intended to be value-free, but it inevitably forces the individual into a static, bounded category which, when combined with the value of "control," ends by degrading the individual who was to be succored.

While there is no way to avoid the value consequences of any philosophy of science or research method, awareness of the particular implications of each choice permits the implementation of the particular view of Man accepted by each researcher. For the field of psychology as a whole, a flexible and open-ended "science" is the only safeguard.

It is the intention of this volume to initiate some questions regarding the values which have been traditionally advocated for the research training of psychologists. Hopefully the ideas presented here will provide some equilibrium to the current positivistic imbalance.

REFERENCES

Szasz, T. S., *Ideology and Insanity.* Garden City, New York: Anchor, 1970.

CONTENTS

Chapter 1

"MENTALISM" AND "ENVIRONMENTALISM"

"...all our science is just a cookery book, with an orthodox theory of cooking that nobody's allowed to question, and a list of recipes that mustn't be added to except by special permission from the head cook."

Aldous Huxley
Brave New World

Psychology, more than most professional disciplines, has been concerned with its status as a science. From a clinical perspective, this solicitous attitude can be viewed as a sign of insecurity, anxiety and defensiveness—suggestive of the extravagance of denial. Psychologists have attempted to imitate an outworn model of nineteenth-century physics. It is time for a reassessment.

Too much effort has been expended in the direction of establishing limiting criteria for what is acceptable within a "scientific" psychology. The consequence is a restrictiveness which continues to have stultifying effects upon theory, method and subject matter. Psychologists are told in advance how they *must* think, act, observe and investigate if they are to remain "scientists." However, while many pretend to observe these "scientific" criteria and outdo each other in attacking transgressors for failure to observe with sufficient compulsion the rituals of this superstition, few actually function according to the required criteria (since it is almost impossible to proceed within such restrictive limits and assumptions).

One of the orienting assumptions of the current "scientific faith" of most psychologists is the exorcism of "mentalism." Why "mentalistic" concepts, theories or even observations must be excluded from psychology is seldom explored beyond the ritualistic incantations of "subjective," "undefin-

11

able," "unscientific," etc. (e.g., Skinner, 1971; Spence, 1956). As a result, internal events such as feelings, attitudes and values—which are *most basic* to our definition as human beings—are dismissed from the field of psychology. If "mentalistic" contents sometimes creep into the psychological realm, a hasty search is initiated in order to find some means to convert them into "safe" external events such as stimulus and response or, at least, to cleanse them by association or direct connection with "observables" (meaning external variables).

Allport (1951, p. 157) has also pointed out this peculiar bias against "mentalism" which is coupled with a failure to view critically the limits of "environmentalism." He suggests that one would be considered unbalanced to speak of "the objective, mechanomorphic hocus-pocus of physicalism." Allport goes on to point out that by sticking to these "peripheral, visible operations" it is taken on faith that the complex issues considered by most of mankind to be our most vital concerns will eventually be dealt with. However, nothing within the realm of current "scientific psychology" suggests that this has occurred. If anything, the outcome has been to trivialize and oversimplify the complex and the meaningful. The very focus of such "physicalism" and "environmentalism" requires the investigator to underplay—and in practice to denigrate—the central, the future oriented and the experiential.

The extremity of this type of oversimplification is found in B. F. Skinner's (1971) writing. The complex issues of freedom have been reduced to "a matter of contingencies of reinforcement (p. 37)"; human dignity and worth have been frivolously disposed of in terms of "preserving due credit (p. 58)." Ramifications of these concepts—whose branches should be traced to hereditary, mentalistic, environmental, sociological, etc. points of view—are restricted to a single interpretation where the entire burden of explanation is supported by a limited set of external influences. Even love is simply "another name for the use of positive reinforcement (Skinner, 1962, p. 300)."

Psychologists *must* come to understand that *whatever*

assumptions and criteria are chosen to define science, they will channel, distort and bias the resulting observations and theories regarding human behavior. This applies to "environmentalism" and "mentalism" equally. The only view of man which can be developed as a consequence of the present overemphasis on the environment, is one which leaves him at the mercy of outside forces. A perfect example of this approach can be found in Skinner's (1971) recent volume, *Beyond Freedom and Dignity,* which reflects a view of man filtered through a Skinner box.

"A culture is very much like the experimental space used in the analysis of behavior. Both are sets of contingencies of reinforcement. A child born into a culture as an organism is placed in an experimental space. Designing a culture is like designing an experiment; contingencies are arranged and effects noted (1971, p. 153)."

Only those behaviors that the "experimental space" permits to appear and develop can possibly be observed and incorporated within the resulting "laws" of human functioning. The prohibitive dimensions of the experimental model will be assessed, in depth, later in this volume; it is sufficient, at this point, to indicate the overstrained metaphorical quality of Skinner's analysis. However, the salient element of this criticism is not to ostracize environmental or experimental positions, but to underline the indispensable need for also taking into account a mentalistic point of view.

Furthermore, a mentalistic perspective focuses upon the subjective nature of all experience. The perceptual process provides the final common pathway for the intake of all information, and this function operates in an active, reconstructive fashion (e.g., Kilpatrick, 1961; Klein, 1970; Piaget & Inhelder, 1969; Solley & Murphy, 1960; Vernon, 1962); perception is not a matter of the reception of objective, invariant, external stimuli. Full understanding of cognitive processes requires an assessment of the mental events which take place during thought. The restrictiveness of limiting observations and concepts to the "objective" and "environmentalistic" leads to such absurdities as the equation of love with positive reinforcement (Skinner, 1962, p. 300). Therefore, since all knowing is, in the long run, contingent upon human experience, even the behaviorist does not deal behaviorally with his own chosen subject matter; he deals with it experientially. One of the difficulties of the subjective approach, as Bugental (1967, p. 7) has pointed out, raises a possible explanation for the motivation behind the rigidity of "objective environmentalism." Since mentalistic methodologies require an unending search using data which may never be fully comprehended, the behaviorist's position may be more of an intolerance of ambiguity and of process than a rational guide required by the subject matter.

Cassirer (1944, p. 16) and Bugental (1967, p. 5), while recognizing that a subjective or introspective approach has its limitations, agree with the position that the ultimate foundations of knowing are dependent upon human experience. Immediate awareness of feelings and thoughts must become a focal point for the field of human psychology. In a similar fashion, Langer (1964, p. 14) has indicated that although methodological limitations continue to discourage contemporary psychologists from dealing with their essential subject matter—mental phenomena, human psychology must be able to deal with events such as symbols, fantasy, religion, self, and morality (Langer, 1967, p. 38). There need be no apology for focusing upon "mind" (Langer, 1967, p. 51). Apologies continue, however, and the tainted is cleansed by means of appropriate ritual (i.e., an appeal to scientism). Skinner, for example, (1971, pp. 3-19) suggests that his emphasis on behavior (external events) is dependent upon the practical issue that mentalism obscures a study of behavior, but his defense of this statement is primarily laced with references to his opinion of what is necessary for a "scientific" psychology.

There are instances, nevertheless, of experimental psychologists who, having found their explorations blocked by a radical environmentalistic tradition, have grasped the necessity for incorporating experiential and mentalistic constructs in the pursuit of understanding certain types of subject matter. As a case in point, Maslow (1971, p. 3) has reported shifting to "mentalistic" methodologies and concepts because he was unable to deal with the psychological issues he was concerned with using the "scientific" criteria prevalent at the time (limitations which still dominate psychological research). He has characterized these restrictive assumptions and methodologies as "behavioristic," "positivistic," "scientific," "value-free," and "mechanomorphic." Other approaches had to be developed. The new assumptions and methods were to be oriented toward an exploration of the depths of human nature (Maslow, 1965, p. 29). He considered the discovery of unconscious motivation to be the single most important contribution to psychology, but pointed out its neglect by many researchers. Maslow (1971, p. 150), therefore, advocated a return to "mentalism" without any qualms about breaking taboos. Not only will psychologists survive offenses against the gods of "objectivity" and "scientism," but psychological research and theory will become more powerful by the inclusion of the "psyche." This deduction has been echoed by Matson (1965, p. 235), May (1962, p. 35), and Rogers (1965, p. 164). However, while many investigators limit their arguments to the value of examining internal events, Von Bertalanffy (1967, p. 10) has questioned the very foundation of "environmentalism" in that even fruit flies and Pavlovian dogs do not fit the behavioristic model. Even at these levels an explanation of individual differences requires a supposition of autonomous activity (i.e., must be concerned with internal events).

There is a growing recognition that subjective and mentalistic concepts are essential for a healthy "science" of psychology although the latter term is usually avoided: Cantril and Bumstead (1965), and Giorgi (1970) emphasizing a humanistic orientation; Hartman (1960) and Horowitz (1963) in regard to psychoanalysis; Murphy and Spohn (1968, pp. 50-67) discussing "The Reality of the World Within"; Rapaport (1957; 1960; 1967a) in regard to his own experiential self-observation and psychoanalytic exploration; Royce (1965; 1967) in relation to symbolic and intuitive explanation; Sperry (1970, p. 588) as part of a reassessment of consciousness in the realm of brain research; and Van Kaam

(1965) in recognition of the inevitability of subjectivity.

In conclusion, I am proposing—in contrast to Skinner, (1971, p. 12)—that the exclusive study of behavior interferes with an investigation of the "mind." However, I am not recommending the excommunication of "environmentalism"; this would emulate the errors which are being criticized here. It is only when "mentalistic" observations, methods and concepts are included that psychological theories will begin to reflect a more comprehensive perspective. The difficulties of understanding human behavior will not be solved by looking away from the whole man, nor will such comprehension be furthered by environmentalistic trivialization. Psychologists must learn to function in terms of a "principle of indeterminacy" regarding their scientific assumptions and methods: all techniques and presuppositions *must be* followed up as each has its own strengths and limitations.

REFERENCES

Allport, G. W., "The Emphasis on Molar Problems," in M. H. Marx (Ed.), *Psychological Theory.* New York: Macmillan, 1951.

Bugental, J. F. T., "The Challenge That Is Man," in J. F. T. Bugental (Ed.), *Challenges of Humanistic Psychology.* New York: McGraw-Hill, 1967.

Cantril, H., & Bumstead, C. H., "Science, Humanism, and Man," in F. T. Severin (Ed.), *Humanistic Viewpoints in Psychology.* New York: McGraw-Hill, 1965.

Cassirer, E., *An Essay on Man.* Garden City, N. Y.: Doubleday, 1944.

Giorgi, A., *Psychology as a Human Science: A Phenomenologically Based Approach.* New York: Harper & Row, 1970.

Hartmann, H., "Psychoanalysis as a Scientific Theory," in S. Hook (Ed.), *Psychoanalysis: Scientific Method and Philosophy.* New York: Grove, 1960.

Horowitz, L., "Theory Construction and Validation in Psychoanalysis," in M. H. Marx (Ed.), *Theories in Contemporary Psychology.* New York: Macmillan, 1963.

Kilpatrick, F. P. (Ed.), *Explorations in Transactional Psychology.* New York: New York University, 1961.

Klein, G. S., *Perception, Motives, and Personality.* New York: Knopf, 1970.

Langer, S. K., *Philosophical Sketches.* New York: Mentor, 1964.

Langer, S. K., *Mind: An Essay on Human Feeling,* Vol. I. Baltimore: Johns Hopkins, 1967.

Maslow, A. H., "A Philosophy of Psychology: The Need for a Mature Science of Human Nature," in F. T. Severin (Ed.), *Humanistic Viewpoints in Psychology.* New York: McGraw-Hill, 1965.

Maslow, A. H., *The Farther Reaches of Human Nature.* New York: Viking, 1971.

Matson, F. W., "Humanization," in F. T. Severin (Ed.), *Humanistic Viewpoints in Psychology*. New York: McGraw-Hill, 1965.

May, R., "The Historical Meaning of Psychology as a Science and Profession," in J. A. Dyal (Ed.), *Readings in Psychology*. New York: McGraw-Hill, 1962.

Murphy, G., & Spohn, H. E., *Encounter With Reality*. Boston: Houghton-Mifflin, 1968.

Piaget, J., & Inhelder, B., *The Psychology of the Child*. New York: Basic Books, 1969.

Rapaport, D., "Cognitive Structures," in H. E. Gruber, K. R. Hammond, & R. Jesser (Eds.), *Contemporary Approaches to Cognition*. Cambridge: Harvard University Press, 1957.

Rapaport, D., "The Structure of Psychoanalytic Theory," *Psychological Issues*, 1960, 2, Monograph 6.

Rapaport, D., "States of Consciousness: A Psychopathological and Psychodynamic View," in *The Collected Papers of David Rapaport*. New York: Basic Books, 1967(a).

Rogers, C. R., "Persons or Science?" in F. T. Severin (Ed.), *Humanistic Viewpoints in Psychology*. New York: McGraw-Hill, 1965.

Royce, J. R., "Psychology at the Crossroads Between the Sciences and the Humanities," in J. R. Royce (Ed.), *Psychology and the Symbol*. New York: Random House, 1965.

Royce, J. R., "Metaphoric Knowledge and Humanistic Psychology," in J. F. T. Bugental (Ed.), *Challenges of Humanistic Psychology*. New York: McGraw-Hill, 1967.

Skinner, B. F., *Walden Two*. New York: Macmillan, 1962.

Skinner, B. F., *Beyond Freedom and Dignity*. New York: Knopf, 1971.

Solley, C. M., & Murphy, G., *Development of the Perceptual World*. New York: Basic Books, 1960.

Spence, K. W., *Behavior Theory and Conditioning*. New Haven: Yale University Press, 1956.

Sperry, R. W., "An Objective Approach to Subjective Experience: Further Explanation of a Hypothesis," *Psychological Review*, 1970, 77, 585-590.

Van Kaam, A. L., "Assumptions in Psychology," in F. T. Severin (Ed.), *Humanistic Viewpoints in Psychology*. New York: McGraw-Hill, 1965.

Vernon, M. D., *The Psychology of Perception*. Baltimore: Penguin, 1962.

Von Bertalanffy, L., *Robots, Men and Minds*. New York: Braziller, 1967.

Chapter 2

THE MYTHOLOGY OF A "UNIVERSAL SCIENTIFIC ESSENCE"

"Facts stay fastened; facts are phantom.
An old one-horse plow is a fact,
A new farm tractor is a fact.
Facts stay fastened; facts fly with bird wings.
Blood and sweat are facts, and
The commands of imagination, the looks back and ahead,
The spirals, pivots, landing places, fadeaways,
The signal lights and dark stars of civilization."

Carl Sandburg
Good Morning America

The *essential point* of this chapter is to assert that a healthy, creative, progressing "science" must be open-ended in terms of its basic philosophic assumptions, theories and methods. The present relativity of "facts" and the indeterminacy of methodologies do not permit exclusive dependence upon a single research technique such as experimentation nor upon one specific set of scientific criteria (e.g., objective, positivistic, environmentalistic). Only a flexible approach to the selection of defining criteria for science appears warranted: a continuous, unremitting, relentless *self-criticism* and *self-questioning* of one's methodologies, observations, concepts, theories, etc., is sufficient. This function, of course, also needs to be supported by *inter-subjective-criticism*. However, openness to evaluation by the scientific community should not be used to attempt to promote slavish conformity. Fromm (1965, p. 23) has effectively described the consequences of an oppressive majority agreement. "Science" *must be* open to many philosophical orientations and assumptions, and *must be* constantly willing to change its point of view in order to deal with new subject matter and new conditions. Psychology as a science *must* provide access for all issues.

The search for a definition of "science" has had a long, controversial and troubled history in the field of psychology (e.g., Bugental, 1967; Giorgi, 1970; Hook, 1960; Marx, 1951; Marx, 1963; Severin, 1965; Welman & Nagel, 1965), and this exploration has led, too often, to prohibitive limitations. Nevertheless, several psychologists have criticized attempts to establish some "universal essence" of science. Rather than begin with a priori criteria, we should observe the way that scientists behave as they go about the business of making observations and creating theories (Demos, 1960, p. 331). In addition, Demos has proposed that flexibility is necessary: science is not the same in all areas and in regard to all problems. In a similar fashion, Giorgi (1970, pp. 11-13, introduction) has asserted that science cannot be limited to one set of philosophical assumptions; it must be sufficiently comprehensive to deal with "the full range of behavior and experience of man as a person." The concepts of natural science are not adequate for this task, and Koch (1967, pp. 433-434) has pointed out that the emphasis has been upon emulating the methods of natural science rather than a determined effort to confront psychology's "historically constituted subject matter." A thoroughgoing "pluralism of ends and means" is required.

None of this criticism should be taken as anti-science; it is a call for the enlargement and flexibility of science, not for its overthrow. The "scientific" endeavor is still one of our main hopes, but psychology as a science must devise methods which are up to the task of studying man's potential. "Scientific psychologists" must realize that they are functioning from the framework of *a* philosophy of science, not *the* philosophy of science (Maslow, 1968, p. 218). The consequence of an exaggerated "natural scientism" has led Maslow (1965, p. 21) to observe that the only psychology books which facilitate an understanding of man are "inexact and unscientific," coming mainly from the psychotherapeutic tradition. This warning in regard to the bias involved in any particular scientific perspective, although apparently heard by only a few, has been repeated over and over again along with the plea for an openness to develop methodologies most suitable for psychology (May, 1962, p. 35; Rapaport, 1960, p. 142; Royce, 1965, p. 23; 1967, pp. 22-27). Seaborg (1968, p. 11) has even suggested a more open-ended position on science than that proposed here (i.e., continuous *self- and intersubjective-criticism*). He has indicated that the essence of research is "the freedom of the scientist to pursue his curiosity." No other criteria are offered in his article for delimiting science. Perhaps this is all that is necessary; however, I feel that this curiosity should be tempered by self-questioning. Yet, there may not be any substantial divergence between the two positions; there is no reason to expect self-criticism to interfere with a scientist's curiosity unless such self-questioning grows out of enforced conformity.

To the openness or pluralism of philosophies of science must be added an evaluation of the consequences of accepting a particular point of view. *Whatever philosophical orientation, assumption or definition of science is utilized, it will in some fashion distort, select, channel, bias, or categorize the material dealt with;* it will heighten the possibility of certain observations, research results, or theories and decrease the potential for arriving at other positions. No single philosophy of "science" can attain the "truth." The healthiest context— that offering the most alternatives, widest perspective and most comprehensive analysis—is a science which leaves itself open.

REFERENCES

Bugental, J. F. T., "The Challenge That Is Man," in J. F. T. Bugental (Ed.), *Challenges of Humanistic Psychology*. New York: McGraw-Hill, 1967.

Demos, R., "Psychoanalysis: Science and Philosophy," in S. Hook (Ed.), *Psychoanalysis: Scientific Method and Philosophy*. New York: Grove, 1960.

Fromm, E., *The Sane Society*. New York: Fawcett, 1965.

Giorgi, A., *Psychology as a Human Science: A Phenomenologically Based Approach*. New York: Harper & Row, 1970.

Hook, S. (Ed.), *Psychoanalysis: Scientific Method and Philosophy*. New York: Grove, 1960.

Koch, S., "Psychological Science Versus the Science-Humanism Antimony: Intimations of a Significant Science of Man," in J. A. Dyal (Ed.), *Readings in Psychology*, 2nd ed. New York: McGraw-Hill, 1967.

Marx, M. H. (Ed.), *Psychological Theory*. New York: Macmillan, 1951.

Marx, M. H. (Ed.), *Theories in Contemporary Psychology*. New York: Macmillan, 1963.

Maslow, A. H., "A Philosophy of Psychology: The Need for a Mature Science of Human Nature," in F. T. Severin (Ed.), *Humanistic Viewpoints in Psychology*. New York: McGraw-Hill, 1965.

Maslow, A. H., *Toward a Psychology of Being*, 2nd ed. New York: Van Nostrand Reinhold, 1968.

May, R., "The Historical Meaning of Psychology as a Science and Profession," in J. A. Dyal (Ed.), *Readings in Psychology*. New York: McGraw-Hill, 1962.

Rapaport, D., "The Structure of Psychoanalytic Theory," *Psychological Issues*, 1960, 2, Monograph 6.

Royce, J. R., "Psychology at the Crossroads Between the Sciences and the Humanities," in J. R. Royce (Ed.), *Psychology and the Symbol*. New York: Random House, 1965.

Royce, J. R., "Metaphoric Knowledge and Humanistic Psychology," in J. F. T. Bugental (Ed.), *Challenges of Humanistic Psychology*. New York: McGraw-Hill, 1967.

Seaborg, G. T., "Goals in Understanding Science," in R. V. Guthrie (Ed.), *Psychology in the World Today*. Reading, Mass.: Addison-Wesley, 1968.

Severin, F. T. (Ed.), *Humanistic Viewpoints in Psychology*. New York: McGraw-Hill, 1965.

Wolman, B. B., & Nagel, E. (Eds.), *Scientific Psychology*. New York: Basic Books, 1965.

Chapter 3

TRADITIONAL "CRITERIA OF SCIENCE"

"...Reason betrays men into the drawing of hard and fast lines, and to the defining by language—language being like the sun, which rears and then scorches. Extremes are alone logical, but they are always absurd; the mean is illogical, but an illogical mean is better than the sheer absurdity of an extreme. There are no follies and no unreasonableness so great as those which can apparently be irrefragably defended by reason itself, and there is hardly an error into which men may not easily be led if they base their conduct upon reason only."

Samuel Butler
Erewhon

In arguing for an open-ended "scientific psychology," what of the variety of criteria which have been so laboriously developed as a safeguard for inquiry? These criteria must be subjected to a new assessment in terms of the fashion with which they—inevitably—modify and limit the observations and theories which they allow to emerge. Perhaps the best place to begin is with the pervasiveness of *"scientism"* in the field of psychology. This involves the assumption that science is capable of solving all problems and of providing unlimited control over nature. The primary underpinning for "scientism" in psychology has been the thesis that research must be empirical, positivistic, reductionistic, quantitative, deterministic, predictive and environmentalistic. The question of radical environmentalism has been examined in chapter one, and the remainder of this section will be dedicated toward a preliminary challenge of other criteria from this configuration of values.

Giorgi (1970, p. 133) has pointed out that "scientism" is not adequate even for the physical world. All understanding of the physical world presupposes the "life world." The psychologist must account for the phenomenological appearance of objects, not how they "ought" to appear (Giorgi, 1970, p. 139). The same principles must be applied to "man the investigator" as are applied to "man as a person" (Giorgi, 1970, p. 202). In a similar direction, Maslow (1968, p. 15) has stated that the inclusion of mental phenomena and experience in psychology requires radical changes in the collection of values traditionally associated with "scientism"; concepts such as parsimony, simplicity, precision, orderliness, logic, elegance, definition, objectivity, etc., are abstractions which may not be adequate for an understanding of raw experience. Even the criterion of verifiability cannot be spared in this reassessment; Polanyi (1969, pp. 53-54) has demonstrated the impossibility of strict verification—"Verification and falsification are *both formally indeterminate* procedures." It is time to outgrow "scientism," and to promote an atmosphere conducive to creative cross stimulation.

Quantification has become one of the overriding proscriptions in the struggle for scientific respectibility. This has led, Giorgi (1970, pp. 64-65) suggests, to "How do you measure?" as the central question of methodology, and attention to the relevant subject matter has become secondary. Psychologists have forgotten how to ask nonmeasurement questions. As a consequence, the bias arises that "a phenomenon *is* to the extent that it is measurable." While disclaimers are frequently made by the naturalistic psychologist, they continue to observe and theorize through the spectacles of such questions, and the only observations and theories which can arise are those which pass this filtering process. Even a superficial perusal of the journals of the American Psychological Association demonstrates the necessity of sophisticated statistical analysis (measurement) as a requirement for publication.

A second major scientific problem is the issue of *definition*; psychologists have given great emphasis to the operational approach in an attempt to resolve the obstacles provided by this question. However, operationalism has become highly restrictive, and is frequently used as a defense of environmentalism. The environmentalistic, naturalistic psychologist continues to suggest that operational approaches cannot be utilized with psychoanalytic concepts. When attempts have been made, psychoanalytic concepts and observations are forced into purely environmentalistic operations; the resulting failure to confirm such concepts is then considered to be an adequate repudiation of the theory. They refuse to operationalize within the psychoanalytic context (psychoanalytic therapy), or are unprepared to do so because they do not accept the psychoanalytic process as a legitimate method. In spite of Rapaport's (1961, pp. 41-110) cautions (originally published in 1942) regarding the difficulties involved in the experimental verification of psychoanalytic concepts, researchers such as Eysenck (1961), and Skinner (1954) continue to oversimplify and misunderstand these ideas. A perfect example of Skinner's failure to grasp the gestalt of psychoanalytic concepts is found in his effort to operationalize the defense mechanism repression in purely environmentalistic terms:

> ". . .behavior which is punished becomes aversive, and by not engaging in it or not 'seeing' it, a person avoids conditioned aversive stimulation (1974, p. 155)."

Even Skinner has recognized that there are also "feelings associated" with this set of conditions, but "the facts are accounted for by the contingencies (1974, p. 155)." Mentalistic operations are considered inadequate, unreliable, etc., as if the environmentalistic operations were solving current problems. The definitions of stimulus, response and reinforcement in current psychology are primarily a result of the experimenter's convenience regardless of what the individual perceives as meaningful in the situation, and they do not take into consideration the total repertoire of responses which are present.

Bridgman (1965, p. 228) did not provide any such limiting conditions for operational analysis when he proposed the conception. He has suggested that an operational analysis is always possible; it is simply an assessment of "what was done or what happened." There are no a priori rules, such as restriction to external variables, nor is it possible to provide exhaustive description (Bergmann, 1965, p. 226). Operationalism provides *a* definition, not *the* definition, and, therefore, it need not be confined to a particular point of view or philosophy of science such as environmentalism. But, Bridgman (1965, p. 228) has delineated another difficulty; operationalism can be pushed beyond the point of usefulness—it can lead to an endless digression of no practical purpose. Operationalism does not replace thinking or theorizing, and it need not be pursued to a point of absurdity (i.e., beyond a reasonable description of "what was done or what happened"). Whatever approach to definition is chosen, however, it will have prejudicial consequences. If a restrictive operationalism is used (e.g., one based upon environmentalism), only those elements which can pass this filter will be defined—whole areas of psychology will be excluded. While certain scientists may, for their own purposes, *require* precise definition, the efforts of some investigators will be interdicted by an insistence upon *any* particular criteria for definition (e.g., operationalism, precision). Demos (1960, p. 330) has indicated that the exact sciences have not handicapped themselves in this way, and quotes Bridgman as suggesting no method other than that of the investigator "doing his damndest." In addition, Matson (1965, p. 234) has proposed that operationalism, like other approaches to definition, cannot escape the fact that it is implemented by a human observer; as a consequence, it does not avoid the possibilities of personal bias. There is no justification for the notion that operationalism cannot be applied equally well to "mentalistic" as to "environmentalistic" observations. All that is required is to specify "how one goes about making a particular set of observations." Such specifications need not be simple or easy.

Even more restrictive than certain forms of definitional rules is the current conception of *"objectivity."* As a required characteristic of scientific psychology, "objectivity" probably represents the most dangerous bias of all of the present day attempts to define *the* nature of science. Even at the simplest level, description and observation, "objectivity" is being propounded from a highly one-sided perspective in current research in psychology. In contrast to this, Maslow (1968, p.

40) has demonstrated the possibility of scientific study with "need-disinterested" perception as well as the focused, "objective" perception promoted in the typical experiment. The former type of perception tends to be less abstract and analytic and more concrete and synthetic. This type of perception (and thought) is characteristic of self-actualizing people. "Less developed people" seem to live in an Aristotelian world of clearly defined, mutually exclusive classes while self-actualizers function in terms of interpenetrating wholes. Even if one does not agree with the superiority of the non-Aristotelian logic of self-actualizing people, Maslow has pointed to the major concern here; our basic modes of thinking, observing and describing are prejudiced toward only one idea of objectivity. For example, every clinician has probably experienced the pernicious and destructive effects of classification upon human beings (e.g., the child classified as stupid by an IQ test or the adult accused of incompetence by such terms as schizophrenia). The value that these terms have applies only to part processes of the individual, but leads to condemnation of the total personality (and causes others to respond to them as if the part represented the whole—a type of thinking usually discussed as regressed or primary process). Here we have a situation where the ideal of logic and therefore the foundation of "objectivity," Aristotelian thinking or categorizing into exclusive classes, leads to dream-logic or pars- pro toto observation, conceptualization, and responding. Objectivity cannot have a single standard since objectivity from an Aristotelian perspective can lead to irrationality, absurdity and destructiveness. The present conception of "objectivity" needs to be modified in the direction of a variety of approaches to observation, description and thought. Once it is recognized that there can be more than one standard for "objectivity," the only requirement necessary is to specify the particular form which is being applied, e. g., Aristotelian or self-actualizing.

The position promoted here should not be viewed as a total attack upon the traditionally developed criteria and controls of scientific research, but it is a declaration of the need for open-ended definitions of objectivity. While for certain purposes it may be considered "objective" to weigh the life of one person versus another, it is just as "objective," from another perspective, to find no possible basis for such a comparison. The death of two friends is not "objectively" twice as bad as the death of one, nor is it even necessarily worse. Therefore, these experiences cannot be put into ratio scale form, and perhaps do not even fit ordinal scale data. Aristotelian logic cannot be the only "objective" basis for deciding human ethics or even the only foundation for behavioral understanding. Maslow (1968, p. 100) has also made it quite clear, however, that his criticism of Aristotelian objectivity does not mean that there is some absolute form of objectivity to replace it. The objectivity of self-actualizers (i. e., B-cognition) is just *one* form of this concept. Each of these modes of objectivity needs the other—they are complementary. Korzybski (1951, pp. 180-200) and Hayakawa (1954, pp. 217-223) have provided a further exploration of the means by which Aristotelian language structures—and therefore distorts—thought. For example, the dichotomy between subject and object in English language forms may require the artificial separation of parts of a continuous process. Maslow (1971, pp. 17-18) has coined the term "Taoistic objectivity" or "love knowledge" to deal with his alternative meaning of objectivity. Loving perception (i. e., that arising in a caring, respecting, accepting, nonmanipulative relationship) produces kinds of knowledge (i. e., objectivity) which are not available to nonloving observation. "Objectivity" should apply to "seeing what is there," not simply to the perspective of cold, rational logic.

Other writers have also dealt with the limitations of traditional conceptions of "objectivity" in relation to observation and description. Cantril and Bumstead (1965, p. 294) have indicated a particular difficulty with applying objectivity to experiential data. They have pointed out that experience, independent of a particular orientation toward description, is almost inaccessible. The very intention to describe and report experience interferes with its "structure" and "flow"

(Cantril & Bumstead, 1965, p. 295). But, their suggestion that description is inevitably analytic and sequential indicates that they are speaking more of traditional modes of objectivity than of Maslow's (1971, p. 18) "Taoistic Knowing." Seeley (1967, pp. 102-103), however, has supplemented Cantril and Bumstead's position by showing that the statement of a "fact" about human behavior when heard affects the behavior and modifies the original observation (i.e., falsifies). While any orientation toward observation will bias reporting, the use of complementary methods can provide the most comprehensive perspective. In this vein, the experimental psychologist could well benefit from the caution which is applied routinely to psychoanalytic observations—continuing scrutiny of the observer's (in the case of experimentation, the researcher's) mental processes during and following an observation, and depth exploration of one's capacity for functioning preliminary to observing in the form of personal analysis (Hartmann, 1960, p. 23). A scrutinization and clarification of one's basic attitudes, feelings, values, etc., toward research and toward *humanity* should be a prerequisite for the training of the experimentalist.

Langer (1967, p. 36) has been even harsher in criticizing the "idolatry" involved in the experimentalist's devotion to "objectivity." She argues against the general rigidity of experimental methodology in that the traditional conception distorts human observations in terms of the "speechless mentality" of other animal forms. Langer's position can be extended to include other forms of misrepresentation such as the extent to which experimental methods fit nonhuman objects (i. e., computers and other mechanical models). In addition, Bruner (1965, p. 5) has spoken of the "fetish of objectivity," and points out its limiting effects upon the preparatory, but critically necessary, thought and writing which are needed to stimulate formal investigation. Finally, Rapaport (1960, pp. 40-41) has demonstrated one of the means by which current conceptions of objectivity have biased the basic assumptions utilized for understanding human nature. Psychoanalytic theory, based primarily on psychoanalysis as a method of participant observation, considers all behavior to be mutiply determined. This principle of overdetermination means that no response can be considered an id behavior or an ego behavior. Every act has id, ego, superego, conscious, unconscious, adaptive, etc., origins. This conception of multiple determination is a direct outcome of the form of observation used by psychoanalysis, and, as Rapaport has suggested, it is not accidental that experimental psychologists have not developed such concepts. The "objective orientation" which isolates, analyzes and separates is not amenable to the uncovering of the point of view incorporated in overdetermination. Once again, it can be seen that all "scientific" assumptions and methods preselect, prearrange and preorganize the data which can be obtained as well as determining resulting concepts and theories.

Another of the rituals of "scientific psychology" is *"control."* While traditional conceptions of "control" offer some guarantee for certain limited developments by the otherwise mediocre, "control" comes in many forms, and any particular approach inevitably precludes some other type. Only an open-ended approach to "control" can prevent methodological hardening of the arteries. Bugental (1963) has pointed out the futility of controlling all of the potentially influential factors other than independent and dependent variables. The assumption that this has ever been done, particularly in research with human beings, is nothing more than pretense. Bugental (1963) has also indicated that this limitation cannot be solved simply through the creation of more tests or greater dependence on computers. What we require is an openness to new perspectives, not just advances in technique within the current orientation. The assumptions that uncontrolled variables are not relevant, that events are randomly distributed, that the form of a distribution is constant from one condition or state of consciousness to another, etc., generally remain—inevitably remain—just assumptions. A variety of alternate hypotheses and approaches can be developed as a foundation for research.

An additional bias of much, but certainly not all, current

"scientific psychology" is an aversion to *theorizing*. While it is not the purpose of this section to suggest that theory construction is a requirement for "science" (since the main purpose is to eliminate limits), it is obvious that the acceptance or rejection of theorizing affects one's observations, methods, philosophy of science and view of man. The compulsion to begin with the "facts" and to avoid theorizing as if "facts" were invariant and independent of subjective reconstruction is a good example of the prejudice which can result— e.g., Skinner (1962, pp. 58-60). As a consequence of the fear of formulating theories, psychologists keep collecting the same "facts" over and over again (Dewey, 1939, p. 254). For Dewey, facts are relatively meaningless by themselves and require theoretical integration. Rapaport (1960, p. 36) has taken a similar position in suggesting that observables by themselves cannot provide a basis for explanation—theory is necessary. In addition, "facts" alone cannot even indicate appropriate methods for observation or measurement. Therefore, the use of theory (or lack of its use) influences methodology as well as the interpretation of the "facts." The extreme empirical position seems to attribute some ultimate "truth-value" to "facts," but "facts" can also be considered constructs which are filtered through the subjective, experiential, perceptual apparatus. Instrumentation does not alter this situation; it just modifies the medium used for transmission to the senses. It is the position of this volume that an integration of empiricism (fact gathering) and theorizing is a more fruitful approach to the advance of human understanding (but not a proscription for "science"). This is proposed with the full recognition that not only the advocacy of theorizing promotes certain selectivity but also any particular theory is necessarily one-sided.

The traditional, American, empiricistic, anti-theoretical bias has been promoted in a variety of ways. One of the primary agencies is what Rapaport (1960, p. 142) has called the "addiction to a single method." By this he means the experimental method and the emphasis upon measurement which has resulted from it. Theorizing, he has proposed, should begin with a solid familiarity with the phenomena involved. The road to theory includes speculation and hypothesis, only some of which can be tested experimentally. Rapaport (1960, p. 143) has suggested that restriction to *the* "scientific method" has blocked theoretical advance in the following ways: training is limited to experimental design at the expense of other methods such as observation; it tends to suppress any openness to conjecture and curiosity; it suggests that experimentation guarantees results; and it leads to a publication policy that obliterates the actual process of research (e.g., it may cover up important unscientific digressions which are a part of *all* methods in practice). No single method is adequate, regardless of modifications and extensions, for the task of fully evaluating human behavior, nor can any single method be offered as the final arbiter of "truth."

One final example of the restrictiveness of current "scientific psychology" deals with *science defined as method.* That is, the definition of science is equated with a single method or a very limited variety of methods—this approach, in psychology, is frequently restricted to the experimental technique. Some of the implications of this approach have already been dealt with in relation to interference with theorizing. Nevertheless, even though most investigators would acknowledge directly or indirectly that they seldom if ever run a research study that closely approximates the classical experimental model, this method is held up as *the* defining criterion of science. In addition, a review of published research would demonstrate that a classical experiment has never been run in the field of psychology. The definition of science by methodology, therefore, not only becomes highly restrictive in terms of the problems that can be dealt with, but leads to hypocrisy and undermines the whole scientific endeavor. Certainly honesty must be more important to science than methodology! The position taken here is that an open exploration of all human experience is the first priority—the problem comes first. Only when an issue is sufficiently delineated should methodology even be considered. "Science" can be better judged by the degree to which it attempts to understand its

subject matter with some scope rather than by allegiance to a
method. Maslow (1965, p. 26) has taken a similar position in
terms of the priority of the issue under study. Definition of
psychology in terms of method turns research into a "sense-
less game." Additional proposals by a number of psychologists place the problem before the method for a variety of
reasons: Bugental (1967, p. 11) has emphasized the need for
psychology to remain human-oriented; Jencks and Riesman
(1968, p. 12, introduction) have suggested that a focus on
method leads to triviality and lack of social responsibility;
Kohler (1947, p. 37) has indicated that the adequacy of a
method should be evaluated in terms of its ability to deal with
the problem; May (1965, p. 183) has pointed out the extent
to which methods are structured by culturally based assumptions; and Rapaport (1960, p. 143) has warned of the tend-
ency to become the hostage of one's own methods such that
the resulting theory can only predict facts which can be
funneled through the particular technique.

"Scientism" is not a viable philosophic foundation for psychology. It can be promoted only as an act of faith which
cannot be justified by any "scientific facts." However, propo-
nents such as Skinner continue to place unqualified faith in
"science":

> "What we need is a technology of behavior. We could solve our prob-
> lems quickly enough if we could adjust the growth of the world's popula-
> tion as precisely as we adjust the course of a spaceship, or improve agricul-
> ture and industry with some of the confidence with which we accelerate
> high-energy particles, or move toward a peaceful world with something like
> the steady progress with which physics has approached absolute zero. . .
> (1971, p. 5)."

Skinner's (1971, p. 25) "science" or "technology of behavior," moreover, is a highly restrictive, biased interpretation
of what is essential to scientific research: e.g., "A scientific
analysis shifts both the responsibility and the achievement to
the environment." Environmentalism is a legitimate perspective for Skinner to explore, but it is an untested assumption.
It is not *the* necessary outcome of a "scientific analysis." As
a result of similar thinking by other investigators, psychology
is circumscribed by a variety of comparable value judgments;

quantification, operationalism, objectivity, control, radical empiricism, and science as method. Other such presuppositions suffuse research tradition in psychology, but the present discussion is sufficient in order to underline the major point of this chapter—scientific psychology must reexamine its basic values.

REFERENCES

Bergmann, G., "Sense and Nonsense in Operationalism," F. T. Severin (Ed.), *Humanistic Viewpoints in Psychology*. New York: McGraw-Hill, 1965.

Bridgman, P. W., "Remarks on the Present State of Operationalism," in F. T. Severin (Ed.), *Humanistic Viewpoints in Psychology*. New York: McGraw-Hill, 1965.

Bruner, J. S., *On Knowing: Essays for the Left Hand*. New York: Atheneum, 1965.

Bugental, J. F. T., "Humanistic Psychology: A New Breakthrough," *American Psychologist*, 1963, 18, 563-567.

Bugental, J. F. T., "The Challenge That Is Man," in J. F. T. Bugental (Ed.), *Challenges of Humanistic Psychology*. New York: McGraw-Hill, 1967.

Cantril, H., & Bumstead, C. H., "Science, Humanism, and Man," in F. T. Severin (Ed.), *Humanistic Viewpoints in Psychology*. New York: McGraw-Hill, 1965.

Demos, R., "Psychoanalysis: Science and Philosophy," in S. Hook (Ed.), *Psychoanalysis: Scientific Method and Philosophy*. New York: Grove, 1960.

Dewey, J., *Intelligence in the Modern World*. New York: Modern Library, 1939.

Eysenck, H. J., "The Effects of Psychotherapy," in H. J. Eysenck (Ed.), *Handbook of Abnormal Psychology*. New York: Basic Books, 1961.

Giorgi, A., *Psychology as a Human Science: A Phenomenologically Based Approach*. New York: Harper & Row, 1970.

Hartmann, H., "Psychoanalysis as a Scientific Theory," in S. Hook (Ed.), *Psychoanalysis: Scientific Method and Philosophy*. New York: Grove, 1960.

Hayakawa, S. I., "What Is Meant by Aristotelian Structure of Language," in S. I. Hayakawa (Ed.), *Language, Meaning and Maturity*. New York: Harper, 1954.

Jencks, C., & Riesman, D., *The Academic Revolution*. Garden City, New York: Doubleday, 1968.

Kohler, W., *Gestalt Psychology*. New York: Liveright, 1947.

Korzybski, A., "The Role of Language in the Perceptual Processes," in R. R. Blake & G. V. Ramsey (Eds.), *Perception: An Approach to Personality*. New York: Ronald, 1951.

Langer, S. K., *Mind: An Essay on Human Feeling*, Vol. 1. Baltimore: Johns Hopkins, 1967.

Maslow, A. H., "A Philosophy of Psychology: The Need for a Mature Science of Human Nature," in F. T. Severin (Ed.), *Humanistic Viewpoints in Psychology.* New York: McGraw-Hill, 1965.

Maslow, A. H., *Toward a Psychology of Being,* 2nd ed. New York: Van Nostrand Reinhold, 1968.

Maslow, A. H., *The Farther Reaches of Human Nature.* New York: Viking, 1971.

Matson, F. W., "Humanization," in F. T. Severin (Ed.), *Humanistic Viewpoints in Psychology.* New York: McGraw-Hill, 1965.

May, R., "Scientific Presupposition," in F. T. Severin (Ed.), *Humanistic Viewpoints in Psychology.* New York: McGraw-Hill, 1965.

Polanyi, M., "The Creative Imagination," in M. Grene (Ed.), "Toward a Unity of Knowledge," *Psychological Issues,* 1969, 6, No. 2, Monograph 22.

Rapaport, D., "The Structure of Psychoanalytic Theory," *Psychological Issues,* 1960, 2, Monograph 6.

Rapaport, D., *Emotions and Memory.* New York: Science Editions, 1961.

Seeley, J. R., *The Americanization of the Unconscious.* New York: International Science Press, 1967.

Skinner, B. F., "Critique of Psychoanalytic Concepts and Theories," *Scientific Monthly,* 1954, 79, 300-305.

Skinner, B. F., *Walden Two.* New York: Macmillan, 1962.

Skinner, B. F., *Beyond Freedom and Dignity.* New York: Knopf, 1971.

Skinner, B. F., *About Behaviorism.* New York: Knopf, 1974.

Chapter 4

THE DECLINE AND FALL OF THE "EXPERIMENTAL METHOD"

"Above all, science will show him that in the world there exist certain laws of nature which cause everything to be done, not of man's volition, but of nature's, and in accordance with her laws. . . .All human acts will then be mathematically computed according to nature's laws, and entered in tables of logarithms which extend to about the 108,000th degree, and can be combined into a calendar. . . .

". . .I should not be surprised if, amid all this order and regularity of the future, there should suddenly arise, from some quarter or another, some gentleman of lowborn—or, rather, of retrograde and cynical—demeanour who, setting his arms akimbo, should say to you all: 'How now, gentlemen? Would it not be a good thing if, with one consent, we were to kick all this solemn wisdom to the winds, and to send those logarithms to the devil, and to begin to live our lives again according to our own stupid whims?'"

Fyodor Dostoevsky
Letters from the Underworld

In addition to the necessity for a reappraisal of the philosophy of science prevalent in current psychology, it is evident —but very much neglected—that one's choice of scientific method can also bias and restrict the data which can be discovered. Every research and statistical technique is based upon a series of assumptions which must be met in order to justify the appropriateness of their application: analysis of variance requires a reasonable approximation to the assumptions that all treatment groups are drawn at random from a single population, homogeneity of variance and normality of each distribution (Lindquist, 1953, p. 73). Even more crucial, however, all methods are grounded upon values which prejudge the limits and potential of human nature. Therefore in view of the need for methodological reform, this chapter is devoted to an assessment of the classical experiment with particular emphasis upon its basic and unavoidable limitations.

Criticism of the experimental method is *not* an attempt to suggest that it is of no value, but, because of its continuing overevaluation, it is purposely selected for examination.

Experimentation can no longer be viewed as the *only* legitimate method or even *the method of choice* for psychological research. Psychologists must outgrow the naive assumption that we are a "new science" and will eventually systematize observations, data and knowledge so fully that everything will become testable by laboratory techniques. It is no longer possible to continue rationalizing experimental failures by a plea of technological immaturity; many conceptions, in general the more important human questions, will *never* be capable of being subjected to experimental validation. Other methodologies can no longer be considered temporary expedients until appropriate experimental techniques are worked out. It is time for new directions with greater effort expended toward understanding the limits and assets of other approaches, techniques that will have to be a part of a continuing research repertoire. With many issues of human understanding, the best that experimental designs will ever achieve is to support or criticize small bits and pieces—this is its inherent nature. Further, laboratory investigations appear particularly sterile for the qualitative analysis of many human experiences such as altered states of consciousness — e.g., the dream hypnosis or delirium. These statements should not be considered an attempt to interfere with any efforts to extend the realm of experimentation by the ingenious researcher, but the status of psychology as a science (or even more important as a profession since no magic should be associated with the term science) should be independent of a particular method. Psychology can be better judged by the extent to which it fosters human understanding than by methodological purity.

The present evaluation is concerned with the classical experiment: the case where one or more independent variables are manipulated, one or more dependent variables are measured and all other relevant factors are controlled. This technique traditionally assumes the following: isolated variables, use of statistical-quantitative techniques, random sampling, an antiseptic environment, a standardized and automatized researcher (who is objective relative to the problem he is studying), a situation where one group (i.e., the subjects) is kept in the dark as to the purpose of the research, an environment where techniques are developed to pretend that the purpose of the experiment is something other than it is, subjects who will accept the role assigned by the experimenter and will not think about the conditions they are facing, an arrangement which focuses upon promoting maximum efficiency in the subject's functioning (i.e., an alert, problem-solving state of wakefulness), etc. The experiment, therefore, implies a particular philosophy of science and of human nature: simplistic, environmentalistic, physicalistic, controlled, manipulative, deceptive, objective and mechanistic (all of these are characteristic of the typical experiment, but they are not all required by the structure itself). Research approaches which may call themselves experimental because they include some but not all of these elements are already going beyond the narrowly-defined experiment which is being examined here. It may be proposed that this is an attack on a straw man, that no one uses this rigid form of experiment any longer: I agree, but would add that no one ever has and psychologists have done a great deal of pretending in regard to the extent to which the ideal type can be approached. The classical experiment has never been run, at least not in psychological research. For example, there has never been control of all relevant factors; there has never been a random sample of subjects (except possibly where the population has been very narrowly defined); and there have never been non-thinking or non-problem-solving subjects (people who didn't decide for themselves what the experiment was about and then decide whether and how to cooperate). An exploration of the limitations of experimental research must go beyond the frequently stated generalization of artificiality.

Some of the difficulties that have arisen in the attempt to verify psychoanalytic concepts by experimental techniques have been discussed by Rapaport (1951, p. 251); the personality characteristics of the researcher need to be studied as it appears that different types of people are equipped for clinical versus experimental assessment; the experiment is not the only legitimate method; and the complexity of the human personality may make experimental study of certain phenomena "entirely inapplicable" or restrictive in scope. Here Rapaport has emphasized the difficulties which are endemic to the experiment for the handling of complex, overdetermined phenomena, and has pointed to the availability of other methods of verification; but, most important, he has proposed that there are personality characteristics which might facilitate or handicap *either* clinical or experimental research. An analogy to the personal analysis recommended for the preparation of psychotherapists could well be added to the training of experimentalists. All data is, in the long run, channeled through the researcher, and his biases (personal as well as methodological) provide limiting conditions for the resulting observations. These influences are especially potent during the preliminary stages of the experiment. Consequently, personal values, biases, prejudices, etc. need to be explored as part of the experimenter's training; failure to do so continues to promote "uncontrolled," "subjective" influences in this "objective" method. In psychology at least, the traditional experimental "safeguards" are not sufficient to prevent the intrusion of personal values. This is particularly critical in regard to the subtle, indirect control which issues from the selection of a research approach.

Rather than guarantee validity, classical experimental criteria such as repeatability can serve to exclude large bodies of information regarding human functioning. Instead of precise repeatability, which does not exist in human beings, Rapaport (1951, p. 259) has proposed "exact recording of varying conditions in order to allow theoretical accounting for the results corresponding to them." The difficulty of providing exactly identical conditions for repeatability is a limitation for all psychological experimentation (Rapaport, 1951, p. 294). Each replication represents some *"variant"* of the original, and the degree of alteration must be considered in terms of its support or refutation of the original. Thus, as with other criteria of strict experimentation, repeatability (one of the cardinal rules) leads to the exclusion of otherwise observable data. It limits areas and conditions of investigation, and, while it may be of value in relation to some issues, it is not a prerequisite for "scientific" verification. To consider repeatability a necessary precondition for all acceptable data leads to the ostracism of all material which is not highly repeatable (e.g., brain injuries, natural disasters, and childhood deprivation) and to the inclusion of only that which is—another filter for "reality" to pass through. If it is true that no experimental conditions are completely repeatable, this becomes a massive stumbling block or leads to pretense. This is, nevertheless, only one of a series of extensive strictures which limit in advance the data which are able to pass through the experimental funnel.

Ethical restrictions provide one of the greatest barriers to experimentation, but manipulation and invasion of privacy influence, in addition to causing possible detrimental effects, the form that the relationship can take between experimenter and subject (Rapaport, 1960, pp. 137-138). For example, a context where one individual intrudes upon the privacy of another is an unlikely situation for the exploration of trust. Rapaport has also asserted that fitting a problem into a laboratory format usually alters the variable in such a way that only some equivalent of the original factor is dealt with (e.g., a threat of death or a proposal of love in an experimental setting is not likely to be given much weight). While it may be possible to establish transformation rules, they could be derived only from broad study involving a diversity of methods. Furthermore, the laboratory experiment cannot deal with issues which exist only as part of an interpersonal relationship between two or more people when the experimenter-subject dichotomy precludes the development of such a transaction. For this purpose, methodology must be broadened to include techniques such as participant observation. It is difficult to see how these conditions can be met without radically changing not only techniques, but basic dimensions of experimentation such as the "objectivity" of the researcher or the "manipulation" of variables and subjects. Human beings will certainly function differently under conditions where they are manipulated versus situations where they participate, are listened to, are cared about, or are respected. The experimenter cannot eliminate feelings and attitudes towards his subjects; the only question is the nature of these sentiments. The traditional researcher does not even ask such questions of himself, or consider them superfluous.

Maslow (1968, pp. 216-217) has gone beyond Rapaport's qualifications and has suggested the ultimate "subjectivity" of all forms of psychological investigation. All research comes out of deeply-felt personal concerns, and it must do so if it is to be meaningful; all research is a combination of "objectivity" and "subjectivity." This "subjectivity" cannot continue to be ignored, nor does proof of its existence wait upon "experimental" demonstration. One need only attend psychological conferences or read the tone of critical articles to become aware—as everyone must be—of the deep involvement, enthusiasm and hostility, engendered by cool, "rational," "objective," "scientific" psychologists when they evaluate each other's work. In spite of this inevitable subjectivity, the goals of manipulation and control make it impossible for the experiment to deal with such issues as "unselfish love" (Maslow, 1970, pp. 11-18). Unselfish love cannot be maintained or cultivated in a dehumanizing environment like the experiment. How can psychologists evaluate concepts of freedom and responsibility within the confines of a method based upon manipulation, deception and control? Fromm (1965, p. 39) has demonstrated that freedom is a basic quality of human existence, but has also defined a variety of ways that men attempt to "escape from freedom." Obviously, freedom is not a characteristic which flourishes under all circumstances.

An exhaustive study of each dimension of the experimental paradigm is required in order to fully explore the assets and liabilities of this method, but one final example of its limitations will be sufficient to establish the need for a reassessment. The experiment is necessarily interdependent with a particular state of consciousness: the basic assumptions (i.e., implicit values) of "objectivity" and "control" tend to promote an alert, focused state. Even where other states of consciousness are investigated (e.g., sensory deprivation), the method utilized for the collection of "responses" promotes vigilant, concentrated wakefulness (e.g., Rossi, 1969, pp. 28-33). Klein (1970) has concisely summarized the problems involved in this situation with regard to perceptual research.

> "Psychophysical studies bring to bear on response a state of consciousness that guarantees an effective *appraisal of reality,* sharp distinctions between wish and reality, the certain and the uncertain. *It is on results in this state that perceptual theorists have based their laws. Very possibly most of the laws so far formulated are valid for this state alone* (Klein, 1970, p. 259)."

This conclusion could be applied to the entire scope of experimental research. How many of the psychological "laws" or principles of learning, perception and motivation, apply to altered states of consciousness? In addition, to what extent can experimentation be utilized to study directly the quality of these altered modes of experience? While some form-variant of the experiment may be suitable, many basic characteristics of the classical method will have to be modified in order to explore the full range of conscious states. A method —the experiment—which, due to its emphasis on objectivity, facilitates one's ability to respond in logical, rational, alert, attentive directions is not prepared to assess the full range of behavior which characterizes the dream, daydream, hypnagogic state, etc. in terms of their potential arrationality and modified alertness. Any response measure (e.g., I. Q. test, reaction time, questionnaire) which demands careful attention or refined discrimination will tend to push a state like hypnosis toward its rational limits, but it will not permit the discovery of the altered time sense or modified reality contact which may be present. The dream mechanisms of condensation, displacement and symbolism (Freud, 1960, pp. 277-425) would not be unearthed by an experimental approach.

Many researchers, as cited in this chapter, continue to describe the limitations and biases of experimentation, but no one has taken the next step which is required: that is, the dethronement of this technique from its place of special privilege and an "objective" evaluation of its liabilities and

strengths. It is *a* method (with variants) which is capable of
dealing adequately with some problems and incapable of dealing with others. Murphy (1968, p. 25), for example, has
pointed out that the use of any method commits one to the
basic dimensions of its structure. The experimental method
commits one to the conception of a universe constructed of
independent variables which are manipulated in order to
create effects upon dependent variables. The consequences of
these experimental strictures sometimes come to light by
comparison of laboratory findings with the non-laboratory
world: Zimbardo (1969, p. 237) has contrasted the ease with
which motives can be elicited experimentally with the great
difficulty of influencing them in the outside world. One of
the primary conditions responsible for this paradox is the
extent to which people are forced into passive-dependent
orientations by the experimental controls. However, in contrast to the experimental constraints, Zimbardo (1969, p.
238) has suggested that people ordinarily think about and
choose a particular course of action (i.e., take an active
orientation). Even within the experimental approach, an
active role on the part of the subjects produces quite different effects than the usual passivity (Zimbardo, 1969, p. 238).
Klein (1970, p. 57) has emphasized similar shortcomings of
the laboratory, and has summarized his evaluation as follows:
"In short, he the subject must perceive on the experimenter's
terms, which exclude private motives and wishes." If these
motives are isolated, the results are spurious; if they are not
the data is confounded. Henry (1971, p. 15, introduction),
like Zimbardo, has condemned the artificiality of the experiment in terms of stripping the "context from life": removal
of the environment drains the situation of all meaning.
Others, like Von Bertalanffy (1967, p. 13) and Sargent (1967,
p. 131), have been clearly pessimistic regarding the possibility
of developing a psychological understanding of full human
potential by means of an emphasis upon quantitative, experimental approaches.

Laboratory researchers have been aware of these limitations, but have done little to modify their basic assumptions

or to dislodge experimentation from its place of special and unwarranted privilege. However, Rosenthal (1964; 1967; 1968) has pioneered one of the most important of the explorations which has been undertaken. He has evaluated the extent to which experimental results are equated with (and possibly influenced by) the expectations of the researcher. Rosenthal (1964, p. 111) has concluded that human beings influence each other in highly effective but unintentional ways, and the processes involved may be so subtle that superficial analysis will overlook them entirely (Masling, 1966, p. 68, has provided additional support for this inference). While this seems to have come as a shock or surprise to many experimenters—and is now producing angry retorts and disconfirmations—there is substantial evidence which confirms this conclusion (e.g., Buck & Cuddy, 1966; Haggard & Isaacs, 1966; Mahl, 1968). Rosenthal's work is laudatory in terms of beginning to subject the experiment itself to analysis, but he does not go far enough. He does not seem to see that part of the way the experimenter communicates his bias is by the very experimental conditions and arrangements he chooses. The communicative nature of physical arrangements, personal space, etc., is well established in clinical and social research (e.g., Hall, 1969; Proshansky, Ittelson & Rivlin, 1970; Ruesch & Kees, 1959); *no* set of controls can avoid this. For instance, removal of the experimenter is a communication to the subject, i.e., the result is a dehumanized (or at least desocialized) environment where one can respond only to things or to people through things. The experimenter who is willing to put people into this type of situation is communicating something about his expectations, not only toward the particular study, but toward people. The second limitation of Rosenthal's work is that he is attempting to study the limits and biases of the experiment looking through experimental prisms. If the experiment is to be evaluated, it must be subjected to approaches other than itself. Otherwise a self-perpetuating circle is initiated. This simply means that the research evaluation of experiments must be comprehensive and utilize as many methods as possible—the same proposal is required for psychological research of all types. The psychological experiment can no longer be considered a simple extension of the methods of physics and chemistry.

While space does not permit a complete exploration of the issues raised here, it is obvious that the previous discussion has not exhausted the ways in which experimental techniques bias, distort, select and order the data which are filtered through them. Orne (1970) has been moving in a highly desirable direction in terms of exploring the "demand characteristics" of the experiment, but this is just a beginning. Moreover, Carlson (1971), has reviewed a sample of 226 articles in order to expose the existing bias in current research in psychology. Most studies use male psychology students, are experimental in nature, involve a single session, and neglect sex differences. Further, there is a general disregard of subject variables, a limitation to a single dimension of group difference, and a complete absence of any examination of the way that the personality is organized in a single individual. While a laudatory effort, even this extensive list of omissions is not complete; it is limited to the characteristics Carlson thought of in his review. Finally, Mogar (1967, pp. 137-138) has pointed out the superficiality of the distinction between treatment and placebo. Since both have effects, it is a question of differentiating forms of treatment, and not one of assuming a contrast between a condition which may affect the dependent variable (treatment) and a neutral event (placebo). In addition, he has suggested that it is typical, in drug research, to include a number of critical issues as error variance. This is characteristic of experimentation in general; the experiment cannot be expanded to handle a sufficient complexity of independent and dependent variables. Even techniques which are considered multi-factor approaches necessitate relatively simple designs. As the complexity of the experimental design increases to meet the demands of human research, control of all relevant variables becomes a farce and crucial categories are arbitrarily assigned to error variance in the vain hope that they will be randomly distributed across treatments (or that they will at least have similar forms of distribution).

In this fashion, simplicity is a consequence of the limitations of experimental arrangements, but when it is found in the results of an experiment it is attributed to the essential nature of human functioning rather than as an outcome of the technique.

The experiment is not qualified to serve as *the* final arbiter of "truth." As *a* technique, it represents one of the necessary items in the researcher's repertoire. When extended and modified, it is capable of even greater scope and significance as a method of investigation. Nevertheless, as long as experimental techniques retain their essential value structure (e.g., "objectivity," "control," isolated variables, deception, and manipulation), they cannot be considered all inclusive. This caution is not required with other research approaches since they have not been invested with similar idolatrous attitudes. *All research techniques are circumscribed by the particular values and premises which are inherent in them.* It is this conclusion which fails to reach the advocates of radical behaviorism. For instance, the equation of science-experiment-technology is found throughout Skinner's (1962; 1971; 1974) writing, and the deification of the experimental approach continues (e.g., Skinner, 1974, p. 229). But the experiment cannot reveal any human qualities other than those consistent with its intrinsic value structure. In fact, this configuration of values appears to preclude the possibility of the experimental technique serving as a means of discovery. While it may suffice to help confirm or disconfirm issues which have been revealed by other sources, no major psychological concept has originated from the experiment.

REFERENCES

Buck, L. A., & Cuddy, J. M., "A Theory of Communication in Psychotherapy," *Psychotherapy: Theory, Research and Practice,* 1966, 3, 7-13.

Carlson, R., "Where Is the Person in Personality Research?" *Psychological Bulletin,* 1971, 75, 203-219.

Freud, S., *The Interpretation of Dreams.* New York: Basic Books, 1960.

Fromm, E., *Escape From Freedom.* New York: Avon, 1965.

Haggard, E. A., & Isaacs, K. S., "Micromomentary Facial Expressions as Indicators of Ego Mechanisms in Psychotherapy," in L. A. Gottschalk, & A. H. Auerbach (Eds.), *Methods of Research in Psychotherapy*. New York: Appleton-Century-Crofts, 1966.

Hall, E. T., *The Hidden Dimension*. New York: Anchor, 1969.

Henry, J., *Pathways to Madness*. New York: Random House, 1971.

Klien, G. S., *Perception, Motives and Personality*. New York: Knopf, 1970.

Lindquist, E. F., *Design and Analysis of Experiments in Psychology and Education*. Boston: Houghton Mifflin, 1953.

Mahl, G. F., "Gestures and Body Movements in Interviews," in J. M. Shlien (Ed.), *Research in Psychotherapy*, Vol. III. Washington, D. C.: American Psychological Association, 1968.

Masling, J., "Role-Related Behavior of the Subject and Psychologist and Its Effects Upon Psychological Data," in D. Levine (Ed.), *Nebraska Symposium on Motivation*. Lincoln: University of Nebraska Press, 1966.

Maslow, A. H., *Toward a Psychology of Being*, 2nd ed. New York: Van Nostrand Reinhold, 1968.

Maslow, A. H., *Religions, Values and Peak-Experiences*. New York: Viking, 1970.

Mogar, R. E., "Psychedelic (LSD) Research: A Critical Review of Methods and Results," in J. F. T. Bugental (Ed.), *Challenges of Humanistic Psychology*. New York: McGraw-Hill, 1967.

Murphy, G., "Psychological Views of Personality and Contributions to Its Study," in E. Norback, D. Price-Williams, & W. M. McCord (Eds.), *The Study of Personality*. New York: Holt, Rinehart & Winston, 1968.

Orne, M. T., "Hypnosis, Motivation, and the Ecological Validity of the Psychological Experiment," in W. J. Arnold, & M. M. Page (Eds.), *Nebraska Symposium on Motivation*. Lincoln: University of Nebraska Press, 1970.

Proshansky, H. M., Ittelson, W. H., & Rivlin, L. G., *Environmental Psychology: Man and His Physical Setting*. New York: Holt, Rinehart and Winston, 1970.

Rapaport, D., "Footnotes," in D. Rapaport (Ed.), *Organization and Pathology of Thought*. New York: Columbia University, 1951.

Rapaport, D., "The Structure of Psychoanalytic Theory," *Psychological Issues*, 1960, 2, Monograph 6.

Rosenthal, R., "The Effect of the Experimenter on the Results of Psychological Research," in B. A. Maher (Ed.), *Progress in Experimental Personality Research*. New York: Academic Press. 1964.

Rosenthal, R., "Covert Communication in the Psychological Experiment," *Psychological Bulletin*, 1967, 67, 356-367.

Rosenthal, R., "Experimenter Expectancy and the Reassuring Nature of the Null Hypothesis Decision Procedure," *Psychological Bulletin*, 1968, 70, Monograph No. 6.

Rossi, A. M., "General Methodological Considerations," in J. P. Zubek (Ed.), *Sensory Deprivation: Fifteen Years of Research*. New York: Appleton-Century-Crofts, 1969.

Ruesch, J., & Kees, W., *Nonverbal Communication*. Berkeley, California: University of California Press, 1959.

Sargent, S. S., "Humanistic Methodology in Personality and Social Psychology," in J. F. T. Bugental (Ed.), *Challenges of Humanistic Psychology.* New York: McGraw-Hill, 1967.

Skinner, B. F., *Walden Two.* New York: Macmillan, 1962.

Skinner, B. F., *Beyond Freedom and Dignity.* New York: Knopf, 1971.

Skinner, B. F., *About Behaviorism.* New York: Knopf, 1974.

Von Bartalanffy, L., *Robots, Men and Minds.* New York: Braziller, 1967.

Zimbardo, P. G., "The Human Choice: Individuation, Reason, and Order Versus Deindividuation, Impulse, and Chaos," in W. J. Arnold, & D. Levine (Eds.), *Nebraska Symposium on Motivation.* Lincoln: University of Nebraska Press, 1969.

Chapter 5

METHODOLOGICAL PLURALISM

"But you tell me of an invisible planetary system in which electrons
gravitate around a nucleus. You explain this world to me with an image. I
realize then that you have been reduced to poetry: I shall never know.
Have I the time to become indignant? You have already changed theories.
So that science that was to teach me everything ends up in a hypothesis,
that lucidity founders in metaphor, that uncertainty is resolved in a work
of art."

Albert Camus
The Myth of Sisyphus

A wide array of alternative research techniques is available,
but most psychologists do not appear to be cognizant of them
in view of the relative infrequency with which they are
utilized as the method of choice. This oversight is primarily a
function of training: experimental designs are typically the
only approaches taught so that investigators are not prepared
to employ other research modes, and, at the same time, the
putative "supremacy" of experimentation is subtly and
profoundly ingrained into the psychologist's professional
identity. The purpose of this chapter, therefore, is to describe
a series of form-variants of optional research methods. These
selections are not exhaustive, but they are suggestive of a
wide variety of methodological possibilities and of the
potential for going beyond the experiment.

1. The Study of the "Single Case"

As with all approaches, the study of the single case includes
a diversity of related forms. The nucleus of each of these
variants includes an attempt to comprehend the intricacies of
a particular human life. Allport (1964, pp. 251-252) has
provided examples of a number of forms of the individual
case study which he has classified within the "morphogenic

method": attempts to fit any record of personal expression with some other response of the same individual, use of personal letters, questionnaires developed for a single individual, description of all the major foci for a given life process, etc. In these examples, the emphasis is upon "subjective validation," and includes the necessity of consulting the subject in regard to his self-knowledge and reflections upon the research. The typical disjunction between investigator and subject found in the experiment is circumvented here, and consultation can be extended in the direction of recent proposals for incorporating the subject as a co-researcher.

The alliance between investigator and subject in the single case method does not exhaust its advantages relative to the traditional experiment. Since the study of unique events is its primary focus, the lack of repeatability pointed out by Rapaport (1951, p. 259) as a limitation to the experimental insistence upon replication does not hinder this technique. In addition, the evaluation of the individual case can help to effect the value of simplicity which is reinforced by the exclusive dependence upon an experimental frame-of-reference. Keniston (1964, p. 60), for instance, has indicated that the richness of individual lives cannot be grasped from the perspective of parsimony. Only an understanding of a multiplicity of variables along with the "overdetermination" of individual acts and the variety of functions served by behaviors, attitudes and fantasies can begin to explore the idiosyncratic integration that can be called a person. The individual case study, then, makes an important contribution to the comprehension of human experience as a result of its unique structural properties (e.g., Breger, Hunter and Lane, 1971; Hilgard, 1965; Maslow, 1968; 1970; 1971; White, 1967).

Because of its intensiveness and depth of exploration, the study of a single individual can provide information which cannot be obtained from the classical experiment (e.g., Maslow, 1971, p. 75). The focus of a case study always keeps the individual in perspective, and is not biased by large numbers of subjects, etc. While this approach is unique,

some of the concepts derived may be verifiable by other
procedures and, thereby, gain further confirmation from
converging methods. However, support or lack of support
must be evaluated relative to the particular procedure used.
With the use of different techniques, supporting data does
not necessarily take the same form and transformations may
be necessary (i.e., reinterpretation or theoretical integration).
Further, criticism regarding the lack of reliability of this
technique is not germane; there is no such thing as unreliable
data—though there may be data where the conditions sur-
rounding their appearance have not been adequately described.
All behavior arising in any situation must be capable of
explanation by a comprehensive theory. By itself the individual case study is not enough (nor can any method stand
by itself); it is only one perspective.

2. "Systematic, Phenomenological and Introspective Observation"

Systematic observation is a form-variant of a whole series
of possible observational approaches. This method can be
oriented toward the single case or toward a nomothetic
evaluation (although the observation of large numbers of
people becomes very complex and time consuming), and
many of the usual assumptions related to experimentation can
be applied. However, most of the experimental arrangements
need not be retained, and the only essential requirement is
the inclusion of reliable recording devices where the data
record is repeatable. No assumptions regarding parsimony,
control, etc. are necessary.

In contrast to the frequent presumption of experimental
superiority, Rapaport (1951, p. 677) has assessed some of
the advantages of observational techniques. While observation
of a naturalistic setting includes a rich variety of stimuli,
experimental control radically reduces the cues available.
Such control may be useful for some purposes, but it can
lead to extreme over- or underestimation of a person's
functional capacity relative to the type of environments
within which human behavior must be understood and

predicted (i.e., the natural environment). If people require a multi-faceted setting for optimum performance, the isolation of variables in an experiment can paralyze action and underestimate the subject's capability. In this case it is not a limitation of ability, but restriction to deprived surroundings which is responsible. On the other hand, a piecemeal sequencing of responses by the experimenter may eliminate the need for coordination by the subject thereby overrating his potential; ability to respond to a series of simple tasks can be confused with the high-level integration necessary for performance in a real-life situation. Observation, which does not violate the natural setting, maintains the richness and hierarchical structure of the environment and the person— this cannot be kept intact by any procedure which isolates, separates, simplifies and controls. A recent example of the possibility of retaining the intrinsic texture and configuration of the environment can be found in Henry's (1971) observational study of personal deterioration within the family context. Nevertheless, systematic recording devices can be used, and subjects can be trained to function as specialized observers (even with observational approaches, however, caution must be used in terms of the risk of distorting the natural context).

Another form of observation is called *particpant observation:* this focuses upon the interpersonal (mutual) interaction between observer and subject. In this approach the observer's feelings and attitudes are studied as intensively as those of the subject; the observer uses his subjective experience as a source of information regarding the state of the other person and the interaction. However, participant observation begins to merge with what will later be discussed as psychotherapeutic technique. Since the research potential of psychotherapeutic methods will be discussed later, this form of observation will not be extensively reviewed at this point. Participant observation, however, does accentuate the need for training in observational skills, a form of instruction neglected due to the emphasis upon experimental designs (Rapaport, 1960, p. 143). Listening and seeing involve proficiencies which are highly deficient in the adult population and usually neglected by the experimentalist; competence warrants training procedures suited to the complexity of the task.

Phenomenology represents another subgroup of observational techniques. This form of observation attempts to "look naively" at the cues presented to the experiencing person and proposes that a good description is capable, by itself, of providing, confirming or negating evidence for theoretical concepts (Koffka, 1935, p. 73; MacLeod, 1958, p. 34). Appropriate questions can be asked only when description begins at the most basic level, "the life-world" (Giorgi, 1970, p. 153). The phenomenological approach allows for an alternate perspective, and permits the researcher to be present in a form that differs from the experimenter, with a different set of expectations and assumptions (Giorgi, 1970, p. 166; McLeod, 1958, p. 34). "Objective" techniques, after all, do *not* remove the researcher; they portray him within a particular framework. Further, Giorgi (1970, p. 168) has indicated that the manner in which the experiment exists for the subject may have little to do with the way it exists for the researcher, and the reference point for understanding has to include the interaction between the person and the environment. The experiment, or any other technique, becomes part of this context. In view of these issues, Giorgi (1970, p. 168) has recommended including the experimenter and subject fully in the research situation. In practice, this requires a relationship between researcher and subject quite different from the traditional experiment, and leads to a co-operative venture which can be analyzed from that point of view (Giorgi, 1970, pp. 203-204). Finally, he has suggested an open-ended design that allows the subject some choice regarding the final procedure.

One of the major difficulties in extending and implementing the possibilities of phenomenological and experiential observation is the threat of being "nonscientific." The investigation of immediate experience, for example, has been detoured by concern with hypothetical variables (Murphy,

1968, p. 29). In addition, Maslow (1955; 1968; 1970; 1971) has been quite clear about the need for new directions in terms of dealing with experiential data: the "objective" researcher has "blindfolded" himself by failing to seek the participation of the subject (Maslow, 1955, p. 5). However, Maslow (1968, p. 8, introduction) has been primarily concerned with alternatives and flexibility, and does not represent phenomenology in its clearest form. He has demonstrated a willingness to use preliminary study, observation or "sheer hunch," and has extended the investigation of immediate experience to include a form of involved, noninterfering observation (Maslow, 1971, p. 17). This methodological conception obviously grows out of his analysis of the B-cognition used by self-actualizing observers. "Loving" or "fascinated" observation is non-manipulative and noncontrolling. The importance of "loving observation" has also been demonstrated by Laing (1969, p. 35) in terms of his analysis of schizophrenia. A fine beginning for exploring the basic dimensions of this approach has been provided by Fromm's (1963, pp. 22-24) discussion of the process of loving, i.e., care, responsibility, respect and knowledge.

Besides Maslow's phenomenological emphasis, Rapaport's (1957; 1967a) conception of consciousness is dependent upon self-observation of a naive, unstructured type, and Singer (1966, p. 14) and Tart (1972) have recommended a greater emphasis upon self-examination and self-experimentation. A variety of other investigators have also emphasized form-variants of phenomenological study: Van Kaam (1965) the phenomenological method; Moustakas (1967) heuristic research; Shapiro (1967) the self as an instrument; Carlson (1971) use of the person's own curiosity and introspective tendencies; Bonner (1967) descriptive phenomenology, self-anchored perception and immediate cognition; Polanyi (1969) creative imagination; and Royce (1965; 1967) intuitive and symbolic ways of knowing. If psychologists are to retain a concern with the appearance of perceptual events, phenomenology remains an essential method. This is not due to any claims of great accuracy, but is dependent upon the fact that no one except the perceiver can describe the experience at all (Allport, 1955, p. 37).

Introspective methods form a related set of observational techniques which overlap with systematic, participant and phenomenological approaches. While no clear line of demarcation can be established between introspection and phenomenology, introspection tends to emphasize training or preparation for observation. Part of the difficulty of defining introspection is due to the fact that it does not represent a single method, but has been utilized in a variety of forms (see McKellar, 1962). Introspection has a long history in psychology, and its importance was stressed by William James (1950, p. 185) who considered it the primary research technique.

The traditional arguments against introspection can be reduced to the essential limitation of all psychological methods: ". . . introspection is difficult and fallible; . . . the difficulty is simply that of all observation of whatever kind (James, 1950, p. 191)." Therefore, the human observer always comes into the picture as a selective factor at some point in the "scientific" process. Discussion of this ultimate barrier to all psychological research does not represent an attempt to return introspection to the status of *the* method of psychology, but it is time for its restoration as *a* method. Cassirer (1944, p. 16) has made a similar point by suggesting that introspective analysis provides the critical data for the very definition of the field of human psychology.

In addition to its value as a means of investigation, McKellar (1962, p. 638) has pointed out that introspection can be used as a check upon the narrow view of "objectivity" espoused by the behaviorists; it can provide safeguards for the experiment by introspective analysis, on the part of investigator and subject, of the laboratory arrangements. In this way, the researcher can obtain important cues regarding the experience of participating in the particular type of environment established, and can check his expectations against those of the subject. This means an introspective exploration, in depth, of feelings, attitudes, etc., on the part of both subject and experimenter. Superficial questioning by an outsider and mechanical compliance with the experimental routines will accomplish little. While there has been some limited attention to these issues in certain experiments, few in contemporary psychology have explored the potential of an introspective analysis on the part of either subject or experimenter.

There are, however, difficulties in terms of applying this group of techniques (as with any methods), and one of the major problems is with the description of the observations obtained (McKellar, 1962, p. 639). These impediments to description are particularly obvious in regard to reports of experiences such as altered states of consciousness (e.g., dreams), but verbal reports which can capture the visual imagery (as well as other primary process characteristics) of the dream are difficult to obtain with any technique. Introspection is oriented toward preparation and training which can facilitate just such reporting. Similar reasoning has led Lipowski (1967), for example, to recommend the use of introspective reports along with observable behavior in the study of delirium. A solution to the problem of understanding these experiences will not be found by failing to explore them, nor can oversimplified, behavioristic solutions lead to anything other than the shedding of most of the meaning from such phenomena. As an illustration of this point, Skinner (1974, pp. 82-86) has reduced the unique texture of dream and fantasy cognition to—doing in the absence of certain events the things which the individual has been "reinforced" to do in their presence.

Introspective, phenomenological, case study and systematic observational methods all can be quantified but need not be. They can all be purely descriptive—it is even preferable for them to begin at this level. *Descriptive methodologies,* however, are legitimate in and of themselves; they can and do provide an adequate basis for understanding and prediction, frequently a more adequate basis than a quantitative analysis furnishes. For example, Jencks and Riesman's (1968) *"The Academic Revolution,"* an avowedly descriptive approach, is a more valuable contribution to the field of education than most quantitative research studies. The complexity of issues to be dealt with in education, as with states of consciousness and other complex issues, requires an extensive, descriptive analysis. The power of descriptive methods has been demonstrated by King (1970, p. 3) where a high degree of predictability has been obtained in ecological studies. The idea that comprehensive description is an important prerequisite for all study is agreed upon by most researchers, but it is also necessary to suggest that this approach is a legitimate method which is superior to other techniques for particular purposes and under specific circumstances. For example, it can function in naturalistic settings and does not require manipulation or control of variables; the experiment cannot avoid either of these restrictions, and, therefore, cannot provide observations from this perspective. The flexibility of descriptive methods makes them accessible to a wide range of events.

3. *"Psychotherapeutic and Interviewing Methodology"*

While the above methodologies, and their form-variants, are derived from a series of contrasting assumptions regarding the nature of human potential (values which are given little attention by the mainstream of traditional experimental research), there are many other techniques that need to be explored in terms of opening up new mediums or new filters for comprehending human experience. One of the most important is "psychotherapeutic methodology." This involves a series of approaches which emphasize functioning in a human (i.e., interpersonal) context. Psychotherapeutic methodologies are based upon the proposition that the potential to be fully human can best be explored in a context which has been described by Erikson (1963, pp. 263-266) as a situation of intimacy, by Fromm (1963) as loving and by Maslow (1968) as noninterfering love. Therefore, we must use, as respectable "scientific methods," interactions between real people which involve issues that are crucially important to both participants. One of Freud's (e.g., 1949,

p. 106) major contributions, although many have not viewed it in this fashion, was to understand the critical importance of psychoanalysis as a research method in addition to its contributions as a theory and a treatment technique. Psychotherapy as a method is not an approach which needs to be superseded by experimentation, but provides a means for understanding human behavior and includes dimensions (i.e., a context) which can *never* be put completely into an experimental framework. Attempts to make psychotherapy more "objective" or "scientific" for purposes of evaluation have lost sight of its unique potential as a research instrument.

It is time to return to psychotherapy (and psychoanalysis) as a legitimate "scientific" method in addition to its value as a treatment technique. This should not be construed as an attempt to build controls, "objectivity," etc., into psychotherapy. *Any* effort to make psychotherapy more "objective" (in traditional terms) or more controlled (in the sense of manipulating variables, control over subjects, etc.)—that is, to make it fit the experimental paradigm—will interfere with its status as a unique method for understanding human experience and behavior. While modifications in the experimental direction may be useful for some purposes, no means of inquiry can be considered a psychotherapeutic method if it breaks two essential criteria: first, a psychotherapeutic technique must give primary emphasis to its role as a helping relationship for the client—research goals are always subordinate; and, second, it must involve a relationship between two human beings who are dealing with issues of critical importance to both. Any alteration of procedure which attempts to exploit, manipulate, etc., automatically excludes the technique from the realm of psychotherapeutic methodology. The unique perspective of psychotherapy as a research approach is provided by its caring, respecting, nonmanipulating atmosphere. One variation of this form of investigation could be called "method psychotherapy," as an analogy to training therapy or training analysis, where the primary goal is self-exploration, but where the individual initiates this interaction primarily in order to become a better observer, self-observer, or experimenter. In this case, the two criteria suggested above are retained—the emphasis is still upon meeting the person's goals and upon dealing with "real," meaningful human issues for this individual. Psychotherapy, therefore, can be stressed as a means of improving the skills of the researcher and as a legitimate, independent, research technique.

One of the main strengths of this "scientific" method is its ability to deal with important human issues; the experiment is almost entirely excluded from this realm. Although the ultimate restriction is ethical—protection from harm and from invasion of privacy—many of the controls and manipulations of the laboratory experiment produce so much artificiality it is nearly impossible for the subject to take the situation seriously.

There are, nevertheless, a variety of unique elements which are contributed by psychoanalysis as a method. Psychoanalysis is first of all an assessment of psychic life, i.e., mentalistic (Rapaport, 1967b, p. 168). However, the most important dimension of this method is its nature as a long-term interaction between two people (Klein, 1970, pp. 16-17; Rapaport, 1967b, p. 196). In addition, it is a technique that is characterized by: free association (Rapaport, 1967b, pp. 169 & 196), assessment of dreams (Rapaport, 1967b, pp. 169 & 196), analysis of defense (Rapaport, 1967b, pp. 169 & 211) and interpretation (Rapaport, 1967b, p. 169). These ingredients and the long-range involvement provide a unique perspective for the psychoanalytic approach in terms of permitting an exploration of the continuity of psychic processes (Rapaport, 1967b, p. 197). For example, techniques such as free association and interpretation may be able to bridge the gaps in experience found by introspective methods. In addition, psychoanalysis grows out of an assumption that human behavior is largely paradoxical or irrational. Consequently, it conceives of the client as a person who wants to cooperate but, at the same time, does not want to, as someone who tries to communicate but is unable to communicate (e.g., Buck & Cuddy, 1966). Finally, Rapaport has added: "The method is

aimed at discovering and eliminating the obstacles to communication. . .verbal, affective, etc., . . .nonverbal. . .(1967b,
p. 203)," and assumes overdetermination (i.e., multiple caus-
ation of every response) (1967b, p. 215). As with all methods,
psychoanalysis is based upon specific premises and is limited
by its idiosyncratic dimensions, but it is precisely these sin-
gular characteristics which provide the opportunity to go
beyond the boundaries of the experiment.

A variety of other authors have also attempted to explore
the unique methodological properties of psychoanalysis (Freeman, Cameron & McGhie, 1966; Hartmann, 1960; Horowitz,
1963; Janis, 1958; 1960; Kris, 1951; Luborsky, 1966). Hartmann (1960, p. 21) has suggested that the psychoanalyst,
like the experimenter, is concerned with an "exploration of
human behavior," but the framework for evaluation is one
which involves mental events such as motivation and meaning.
In this way, as with Rapaport (1967b, p. 168), he has stressed
the potential of this method for dealing with mentalistic
constructs and data. Hartmann (1960, p. 22) has gone on to
emphasize the merits of the psychoanalytic technique for
dealing with the single case (a large number of observations
rather than many subjects), and the unique nature of the
relationship which includes the advantage of tapping many
layers of personality in both subject and observer. This
participant observation provides, but should not confuse, the
feelings and thoughts of observer and observed. An additional
asset to this technique is its ability to mobilize efforts toward
self-revelation in order to overcome resistance (Hartmann,
1960, pp. 25-26). Of course, this assumes that people do
avoid revealing themselves—or are unable to do so. Most
experimentalists seem to make similar assumptions in terms
of the way that they arrange the setting or instructions, but
the usual solution is limited to some form of trickery or
deception. Finally, Hartmann (1960, pp. 31-34) has pointed
out that the organismic, holistic orientation which underlies
psychoanalytic theory makes it difficult to define clear-cut
independent, dependent and intervening variables. This
obstacle, along with all of the unique characteristics of this

method, makes experimental verification unlikely. Each method provides a different set of lenses, and one cannot automatically shift from one to the other.

Kris (1951, p. 332), like Rapaport and Hartmann, has emphasized the importance of the interpersonal character-istics of psychotherapy. The psychoanalytic observer attempts to fulfill three functions: he records the behavior and feelings of the observer and the observed, and then intervenes in an attempt to effect the interaction. The psychoanalytic inter-view provides a research technique that can be described in terms of its basic elements. It allows the time for testing long-range predictions, and provides a situation, during each session, for the exploration of a large number of hypotheses (Kris, 1951, pp. 338-339). Rules of procedure can also be specified for confirming or rejecting predictions. Kris (1951, pp. 338-339) has suggested sudden insight and the production of new details as means of confirmation.

Janis (1960, p. 166) has provided a more extensive set of criteria (or confirming rules of procedure) for the assessment of the therapist's hypotheses. For example, the adequacy of predicting a particular childhood experience can be assessed by: free recall of the event during the interview, behavioral communications supporting the genuineness of the experience, independent confirmation from records or relatives, internal consistency of memories, symbolic evidence obtained previous to the therapist's intervention, associations which support the occurrence of the event after intervention, the extent that this situation corresponds with the entire case study, and the observer's clinical judgment of adequacy. While this list is not exhaustive and includes criteria with different degrees of reliability, it does indicate the possibility of providing "vali-dation." But, this is validation within the limits of the psychoanalytic method, and is based upon an assumption of overlapping and non-independent events. These criteria can increase or decrease the reliability of the hypothesis. Janis (1960, p. 178), at a later point, has even added the possibility of using a form of "repeatability" as a confirmatory tech-nique. The continuity of the relationship permits repetitive observations of attempts to deal with a particular type of situation, i.e., particular attitudes and actions displayed in daily life, and sequences of affective and verbal responses during the interviews. Obviously this does not mean repeatability in the strict sense, because no events ever recur in the exact form in which they originally appeared; this conclusion applies equally well to the experiment.

Psychotherapeutic, and interviewing, techniques can be applied to a variety of situations such as creativity (Barron, 1972), hypnotic investigation (Hilgard, 1965; Hilgard, 1970), experiential reaction to atomic warfare (Lifton, 1967) and momentary forgetting (Luborsky, 1966). It is necessary, nevertheless, to explore in depth other issues regarding psychotherapeutic, interview (depth), or interpersonal techniques, and some investigators have already been moving in this direction. Mogar (1967, p. 139) has discussed the conception that the psychotherapeutic process is multifaceted, and is distorted by attempting to isolate it into single variables. The integrity of this process must be retained in order to assess the total configuration. In addition, Jourard (1967, p. 109) has indicated that only certain human potentials will be revealed in the typical, impersonal, research arrangements, but it is possible to develop interactions in which people are mutually revealing. Human functioning is qualitatively different in an environment that includes open, honest exchange than it is in an aseptic, deceptive laboratory. A variant of therapeutic methodology—mutual disclosure— can offer such openness for both observer and subject (Jourard, 1971, pp. 16-17). The promise of this approach has been amply demonstrated by Buck and Kramer (1973; 1974) in terms of their assessment of creativeness in the deaf and the emotionally impaired. Finally, Otto (1967) has proposed another form-variant in regard to his evaluation of "Minerva experiences." The subjects decide in a group-dynamic interaction whether they will participate in the research. This seems to be generally within the psychotherapeutic methodologies. These variants of psychotherapeutic technique are capable of exploring the full range of states of consciousness (i.e., dreaming to waking experience), and include unique properties for dealing with a frequent dilemma of laboratory methods—the unwillingness and inability (due to defensiveness) of people to cooperate with the research venture. It is a primary goal of psychotherapy to deal with these issues, and it is unlikely that they can be resolved (not controlled) in any environment which does not focus upon caring and respecting.

4. New Paths for "Scientific Psychology"

The foregoing discussion is not considered to be all-inclusive, and is intended only to provide some direction for methodological expansion. A further area involves the use of questionnaires, ratings, and scales for the assessment of experiential constructs and observations. The work of investigators such as Breger, Hunter and Lane (1971), Hall and Van de Castle (1966), Hilgard (1965), Tart (1971) and Wessman and Ricks (1966) exemplify the merits of this direction, but these approaches are sufficiently common and well accepted to make it unnecessary to provide a justification of their value here.

Finally, psychologists need to overcome their professional parochialism in order to make greater use of literary and poetic sources. Many attempts have been made to analyze literature and to employ it as a source of stimulation, but literary analysis as an independent research method should be seriously explored. Koch (1969, p. 253) and Royce (1965, p. 23) are the only investigators, that I am aware of, who have made a similar proposal: a recommendation that would legitimize the use of approaches typical of the humanities as psychological techniques. The establishment of such a research method (and an exploration of its assets and liabilities) would mean the use of literary expression as a source of human understanding. One of the primary gains would be to profit by the experience of people who devote their life to developing a facility with language, a skill poorly developed in most psychologists.

Poetic expression offers a form of word usage which can overcome some of the limitations of words (e.g., abstraction or categorical boundaries which make them unfit for dealing adequately with process) for describing and capturing feeling and experience; this has particular relevance, for instance, to observations of altered states of consciousness. In addition, Royce (1965, pp. 23-24) had emphasized the validity of symbolic knowledge and its potential for dealing with "one-to-many correspondences." Openness to the use of symbols, which also reveal the "truth," can make psychology more accessible to the methods of the humanities and more able to deal with the complexity of human experience. Cantril and Bumstead (1965, pp. 293-294) have emphasized the need to utilize literature as a source of insights regarding human nature and as a technique for grasping descriptive experience. For example, poetry provides a synthetic capacity that is difficult to achieve by "scientific methods." The analytic emphasis in most "scientific" approaches interferes with synthesis and integration. Bruner (1965), Maddi (1970) and Wilson (1964) are examples of investigators who have given serious attention to literature as a source of human understanding, but they have only begun to tap the advantages of this approach for psychological research.

In conclusion, while the experimental method continues to reign as a sovereign power in American psychology, a variety of other research paradigms are available. Many of these alternative techniques have been discussed and utilized by investigators, but, even where such approaches have been employed, they are normally intertwined with the network of values advanced by the behavioristic-positivistic tradition— i.e., "objectivity," "control," "simplicity," etc. The advocacy of optional methods is not sufficient. The present reexamination is an attempt to demonstrate the need for a variety of research modes which are coequal with the experiment and are derived from a modified set of fundamental premises (e.g., "overdetermination," "loving objectivity" or "researcher-subject mutuality").

REFERENCES

Allport, F. H., *Theories of Perception and the Concept of Structure.* New York: Wiley, 1955.

Allport, G. W., "The General and the Unique in Psychological Science," in E. A. Southwell, & M. Merbaum (Eds.), *Personality: Readings in Theory and Research.* Belmont, California: Wadsworth, 1964.

Barron, F., *Artists in the Making.* New York: Seminar Press, 1972.

Bonner, H., "The Proactive Personality," in J. F. T. Bugental (Ed.), *Challenges of Humanistic Psychology.* New York: McGraw-Hill, 1967.

Breger, L., Hunter, I., & Lane, R. W., "The Effect of Stress on Dreams," *Psychological Issues,* 1971, 7, Monograph 27.

Bruner, J. S., *On Knowing: Essays for the Left Hand.* New York: Atheneum, 1965.

Buck, L. A., & Cuddy, J. M., "A Theory of Communication in Psychotherapy," *Psychotherapy: Theory, Research and Practice,* 1966, 3, 7-13.

Buck, L. A., & Kramer, A., "Opening New Worlds to the Deaf and the Disturbed," in J. J. Leedy (Ed.), *Poetry the Healer.* Philadelphia: Lippincott, 1973.

Buck, L. A., & Kramer, A., "Poetry as a Means of Group Facilitation," *Journal of Humanistic Psychology,* 1974, 14, 57-71.

Cantril, H., & Bumstead, C. H., "Science, Humanism, and Man," in F. T. Severin (Ed.), *Humanistic Viewpoints in Psychology.* New York: McGraw-Hill, 1965.

Carlson, R., "Where Is the Person in Personality Research?" *Psychological Bulletin,* 1971, 75, 203-219.

Cassirer, E., *An Essay on Man.* Garden City, New York: Doubleday, 1944.

Erikson, E. H., *Childhood and Society,* 2nd ed. New York: Norton, 1963.

Freeman, T., Cameron, J. L., & McGhie, A., *Studies on Psychosis.* New York: International Universities Press, 1966.

Freud, S., *An Outline of Psychoanalysis.* New York: Norton, 1949.

Fromm, E., *The Art of Loving.* New York: Bantam, 1963.

Giorgi, A., *Psychology as a Human Science: A Phenomenologically Based Approach.* New York: Harper & Row, 1970.

Hall, C. S., & Van de Castle, R. L., *The Content Analysis of Dreams.* New York: Appleton—Century-Crofts, 1966.

Hartmann, H., "Psychoanalysis as a Scientific Theory," in S. Hook (Ed.), *Psychoanalysis: Scientific Method and Philosophy.* New York: Grove, 1960.

Hilgard, E. R., *Hypnotic Susceptibility.* New York: Harcourt, Brace & World, 1965.

Hilgard, J. R., *Personality and Hypnosis: A Study of Imaginative Involvement.* Chicago: University of Chicago Press, 1970.

Horowitz, L., "Theory Construction and Validation in Psychoanalysis," in M. H. Marx (Ed.), *Theories in Contemporary Psychology.* New York: Macmillan, 1963.

James, W., *The Principles of Psychology,* Vol I. New York: Dover, 1950.

Janis, I. L., *Psychological Stress.* New York: Wiley, 1958.

Janis, I. L., "The Psychoanalytic Interview as an Observational Method," in G. Lindzey (Ed.), *Assessment of Human Motives.* New York: Grove, 1960.

Jencks, C., & Riesman, D., *The Academic Revolution.* Garden City, New York: Doubleday, 1968.

Jourard, S. M., "Experimenter-Subject Dialogue: A Paradigm for a Humanistic Science of Psychology," in J. F. T. Bugental (Ed.), *Challenges of Humanistic Psychology.* New York: McGraw-Hill, 1967.

Jourard, S. M., *The Transparent Self,* Rev. Ed. New York: Van Nostrand Reinhold, 1971.

Keniston, K., "Inburn: An American Ishmael," in R. W. White (Ed.), *The Study of Lives.* New York: Atherton, 1964.

King, J. A., "Ecological Psychology: An Approach to Motivation," in W. J. Arnold, & M. M. Page (Eds.), *Nebraska Symposium on Motivation.* Lincoln: University of Nebraska Press, 1970.

Klein, G. S., *Perception, Motives and Personality.* New York: Knopf, 1970.

Koch, S., "Value Properties," in M. Grene (Ed.), "Toward a Unity of Knowledge," *Psychological Issues,* 1969, 6, Monograph 22.

Koffka, K., *Principles of Gestalt Psychology.* New York: Harcourt, Brace, 1935.

Kris, E., "Psychoanalytic Propositions," in M. H. Marx (Ed.), *Psychological Theory.* New York: Macmillan, 1951.

Laing, R. D., *The Divided Self.* New York: Pantheon, 1969.

Lifton, R. J., *Death in Life.* New York: Random House, 1967.

Lipowski, Z. J., "Delirium, Clouding of Consciousness and Confusion," *Journal of Nervous and Mental Disease,* 1967, 145, 227-255.

Luborsky, L., "Momentary Forgetting During Psychotherapy and Psychoanalysis: A Theory and Research Method," in R. R. Holt (Ed.), *Motives and Thought: Psychoanalytic Essays in Honor of David Rapaport,* New York: International Universities Press, 1966.

McKellar, P., "The Method of Introspection," in J. Scher (Ed.), *Theories of the Mind.* New York: Free Press, 1962.

MacLeod, R. B., "The Phenomenological Approach to Social Psychology," in R. Tagiuri, & L. Petrullo (Eds.), *Person Perception and Interpersonal Behavior.* Stanford, California: Standford University Press, 1958.

Maddi, S. R., "The Search for Meaning," in W. J. Arnold, & M. M. Page (Eds.), *Nebraska Symposium on Motivation.* Lincoln: University of Nebraska Press, 1970.

Maslow, A. H., "Deficiency Motivation and Growth Motivation," in M. R. Jones (Ed.), *Nebraska Symposium on Motivation.* Lincoln: University of Nebraska Press, 1955.

Maslow, A. H., *Toward a Psychology of Being,* 2nd ed. New York: Van Nostrand Reinhold, 1968.

Maslow, A. H., *Religions, Values and Peak-Experiences.* New York: Viking, 1970.

Maslow, A. H., *The Farther Reaches of Human Nature.* New York: Viking, 1971.

Mogar, R. E., "Psychedelic (LSD) Research: A Critical Review of Methods and Results," in J. F. T. Bugental (Ed.), *Challenges of Humanistic Psychology.* New York: McGraw-Hill, 1967.

Moustakas, C., "Heuristic Research," J. F. T. Bugental (Ed.), *Challenges of Humanistic Psychology.* New York: McGraw-Hill, 1967.

Murphy, G., "Psychological Views of Personality and Contributions to Its Study," in E. Norbeck, D. Price-Williams, & W. M. McCord (Eds.), *The Study of Personality.* New York: Holt, Rinehart & Winston, 1968.

Otto, H. A., "The Minerva Experience: Initial Report," in J. F. T. Bugental (Ed.), *Challenges of Humanistic Psychology.* New York: McGraw-Hill, 1967.

Polanyi, M., "The Creative Imagination," in M. Grene (Ed.), "Toward a Unity of Knowledge," *Psychological Issues,* 1969, 6, No. 2, Monograph 22.

Rapaport, D., "Footnotes," in D. Rapaport (Ed.), *Organization and Pathology of Thought.* New York: Columbia University, 1951.

Rapaport, D., "Cognitive Structures," in H. E. Gruber, K. R. Hammond, & R. Jessor (Eds.), *Contemporary Approaches to Cognition.* Cambridge: Harvard University Press, 1957.

Rapaport, D., "The Structure of Psychoanalytic Theory," *Psychological Issues,* 1960, 2, No. 2, Monograph 6.

Rapaport, D., "States of Consciousness: A Psychopathological and Psychodynamic View," in *The Collected Papers of David Rapaport,* New York: Basic Books, 1967 (a).

Rapaport, D., "The Scientific Methodology of Psychoanalysis," in *The Collected Papers of David Rapaport.* New York: Basic Books, 1967 (b).

Royce, J. R., "Psychology at the Crossroads Between the Sciences and the Humanities," in J. R. Royce (Ed.), *Psychology and the Symbol.* New York: Random House, 1965.

Royce, J. R., "Metaphoric Knowledge and Humanistic Psychology," in J. F. T., Bugental (Ed.), *Challenges of Humanistic Psychology.* New York: McGraw-Hill, 1967.

Shapiro, S. B., "Myself as an Instrument," in J. F. T. Bugental (Ed.), *Challenges of Humanistic Psychology.* New York: McGraw-Hill, 1967.

Singer, J. L., *Daydreaming.* New York: Random, 1966.

Skinner, B. F., *About Behaviorism.* New York: Knopf, 1974.

Tart, C. T., *On Being Stoned: A Psychological Study of Marijuana Intoxication.* Palo Alto, California: Science and Behavior Books, 1971.

Tart, C. T., "States of Consciousness and State-Specific Sciences," *Science,* 1972, 176, 1203-1210.

Van Kaam, A.L., "Assumptions in Psychology," in F. T. Severin (Ed.), *Humanistic Viewpoints in Psychology.* New York: McGraw-Hill, 1965.

Wessman, A. E., & Ricks, D. F., *Mood and Personality.* New York: Holt, Rinehart & Winston, 1966.

White, R. W., "Sense of Interpersonal Competence," in R. W. White (Ed.), *The Study of Lives.* New York: Atherton, 1964.

Wilson, R. N., "Albert Camus: Personality, as Creative Struggle," in R. W. White (Ed.), *The Study of Lives.* New York: Atherton, 1964.

Chapter 6

THE PLACE OF VALUE IN THE FUTURE
OF PSYCHOLOGICAL RESEARCH

"... You shall no longer take things at second or third
hand, nor look through the eyes of the dead, nor
feed on the spectres in books,
You shall not look through my eyes either, nor take
things from me,
You shall listen to all sides and filter them from your
self."

Walt Whitman
Song of Myself

"Science" must be unfettered by any proscriptions intended to circumscribe its realm. In order to implement this
proposition, defining criteria must be reduced to an indispensable minimum, and research methods must be infinitely
expanded. The former requirement can be satisfied by an
enduring critical attitude which does not blight the imagination; the latter need can be promoted by methodological
pluralism.

The conception of limiting and biasing effects of a particular philosophy of science makes it necessary to evaluate
the basic assumptions that one utilizes and the values em-
bedded in them. The primary assumption advanced in this
volume, that *"science" must be open-ended,* is intended to
promote the value of inclusiveness and comprehensiveness. It
is designed to encourage creativity and foster the exploration
of wider and wider ranges of human behavior and experience.

While the discussion of essential criteria could be ended
with the promotion of an unbounded science, it is evident
that any particular investigator will function within a unique
gestalt of values—all assumptions cannot be adopted simul-
taneously. Therefore, complimentary to the openness of

science is the necessity of a *continuing self-and-intersub-jective-criticism*.   At no point can an observation, datum, description, concept or theory be considered validated. Validation is a continuous process, but one that contains different degrees of certainty. Consequently, this axiom is consistent with a conception of the relativity of truth required as a modus operandi for scientific investigation.

Opposition to an absolutist position in science, in addition to providing an opportunity for individual directions, is aimed toward the value of promoting comprehensiveness in regard to the understanding of human potential. One step in this direction can be accomplished by blending an empirical emphasis (which has no necessary relationship to the experiment) with theoretical development.   Facts and low-level concepts cannot stand by themselves; there is no rationale for future directions without theory. If one looks at theoretical concepts, it is possible to assess the values which underlie research.   Without theoretical development it is likely that these values will remain unstated (if they are specified theory development has begun—at least in the direction of a world view or philosophy of man).

Inclusiveness can be additionally cultivated by the acceptance of intrapsychic, mentalistic processes and structures as legitimate research directions with the intention of combining mentalism with environmentalism.   The internal and experiential must be merged with the behavioral (in the traditional sense). This goal can be immeasurably advanced by a return to the study of conscious experience.

A final aspect of promoting comprehensiveness involves working toward the repeal of the "law" of parsimony (at least as most psychologists seem to interpret it). The basic assumption advanced here is that *human beings are extremely complex* (for practical purposes, unlimited complexity), and only theories capable of reflecting human behavior with sufficient depth and breadth and methods capable of investigating multi-dimensional observations will be able to explore this assumption. The classical experiment and behavioristic theories—geared toward simplicity and atomistic analysis—

are incapable of dealing with the totality of human experience. Only a comprehensive evaluation utilizing a diversity of approaches can explore the full range of man's potential. One subcategory of this assumption can be fulfilled by the psychoanalytic doctrine of overdetermination. That is, any behavior must be understood as the intricate end-product of a multiplicity of determinants. This conclusion, and the methodological difficulties it produces, may be lamented, but should not be ignored as a possibility. In addition, the promotion of complexity means that definitions of concepts must go beyond the Aristotelian limitations of mutually exclusive categories. We must learn to utilize categories and definitions capable of dealing with process even though Western linguistic structure is not well adapted to this task. Finally, a third aspect of this assumption involves a need to promote the organismic viewpoint that all elements of personality are parts—artificially isolated—of a total system. This means that if we utilize methods which fragmentize the person, we must eventually put these pieces together into a totally functioning human being. Accordingly, a position like psychoanalysis should be utilized so that concepts can eventually be integrated within a wholistic theory. William James' (1953, p. 204-205) criticism of the "law of parsimony" remains as relevant today as in the past: as an exclusive law of the mind it will end by "blighting the development of the intellect itself quite as much as that of the feelings or the will."

Given the need for scientific flexibility, pragmatism provides an advantageous starting point. As James has pointed out, however, pragmatism is not a theory or a limiting rule, it is merely a facilitating way of "playing the game of science." The "Pragmatic Rule" indicates that the meaning of a concept can always be found either in terms of the concrete item which is designated or in terms of some "sensible difference" which its truth will make to someone (James, 1953, p. 82). In this sense, anything becomes "real" which requires a response (internal or external) from us (James, 1953, p. 92). This orientation can help avoid meaningless philosophical arguments regarding "reality." Frequently discussions of "factual reality" have led, in psychology, to the acceptance of external events as real while internal processes are considered unreal. However, the pragmatic position makes it clear that concepts can be as "real" as percepts, and, therefore, images, thoughts, fantasies and all internal events warrant the status "real" as long as they require the individual to take account of them in some fashion. However, this frame-of-reference, and it is only a means of approach (James, 1955, p. 46), eliminates any "pretense of finality of truth" (James, 1955, p. 45). Finally, pragmatism does not interfere with theory construction; it merely requires that any abstractions facilitate dealing with particulars (James, 1955, p. 57). The pragmatic approach, which is clearly not a restriction to the practical in the usual sense, comes like a breath of fresh air after the stultifying rigidity of behaviorism. It opens up the possibility of the study of experience, of values, of religion, of magic and superstition, etc., since these beliefs certainly make a difference to the individual involved.

Only with a pluralism of methodologies can the above propositions and a full exploration of behavior and experiences be implemented. Oppenheimer (1965, p. 215) has also pleaded for methodological alternatives, but limits this recommendation to the preliminary stages of the development of a science. While his proposal is in the right direction, it does not go far enough. Pluralism is necessary as a continuing element of scientific methodology. There should not be any point, at least in psychology, where methodology is restricted (for example, to classical experimentation). The experimental method will never be capable of dealing adequately with the understanding of full human potential. It will always have its limitations as well as its strengths as a particular method. As Allport (1964, p. 252) has stated, however, psychologists have been considerably more flexible in their models and theories than in their methods. The richness of human experience requires the creative exploration of new approaches to research. The psychologist's task calls for methods which: include the "subjects" as cooperative members of the research team as well as the present exclusion, manipulation and secretiveness; evaluate the attitudes and values of the "experimenter" as well as the "subject"; explore alternate states of consciousness on their own terms not just from the perspective of alert wakefulness; deal with subjective experience itself not just its simplest external manifestations; etc.

The methods of investigation that we use can shackle or liberate the theories and view of man which can evolve. We must use procedures which are relevant to our conception of human potential because the only information, data or observations we can obtain are the ones which pass the filter of our methods. This filter is not neutral; it acts as a medium (Klein, 1970, pp. 66-73; Heider, 1959, pp. 1-34) and distorts and rearranges even what it allows to pass—much is not passed at all. No "scientific" techniques are value-free; the only choice available is either the intentional selection of the values which will be implanted or the abandonment of this option to the mindless vagaries of arbitrary subjectivity. We should attempt to develop a plethora of techniques, and give priority to those designs which permit the depth, complexity and wealth of human experience to be unveiled. It is likely that case study, observational, therapeutic, and other methods described above can be at least as fruitful as experimental arrangements for the exploration of human behavior, and it is evident that they are superior to laboratory designs in regard to a qualitative analysis of human experience.

The implications of these conclusions are not restricted to an exploration of scientific criteria and methods: they extend to society in general. Psychologists have not yet come to terms with the "fact" that values are inextricably interwoven with their techniques, research results and theories. Failure to understand the value-implications of experimental and behavioristic procedures had led to disillusionment and antagonism, but, even more important, it will lead to disasterous consequences for society. Von Bertalanffy, for example, has vigorously attacked the contemporary scene:

"...a large part of modern psychology is a sterile and pompous scholasticism which, with the blinders of preconceived notions or superstitions on its nose, doesn't see the obvious; which covers the triviality of its results and ideas with a preposterous language bearing no resemblance either to normal English or normal scientific theory; and which provides modern society with the techniques for the progressive stultification of mankind (Von Bertalanffy, 1967, p. 6)."

This pessimistic assessment in regard to the present directions of psychology is not limited to Von Bertalanffy.

"In short, if one truly believes that humans should not manipulate other humans, then it seems to be absurd to build a human science on the basis of a paradigm that violates the essential point (Giorgi, 1970, p. 204)."

The most frightening implications of all, however, have been probed by Maslow (1971) and Fromm (1964; 1971). Maslow (1971) has concluded that the consequence of physicalistic, positivistic, manipulative environmentalism is mindless rationality and totalitarianism:

"Many people are beginning to discover that the physicalistic, mechanistic model was a mistake and that it has led us. . .where? To atom bombs. To a beautiful technology of killing, as in the concentration camps. To Eichmann. An Eichmann cannot be refuted with a positivistic philosophy of science. . . .

"He didn't know what was wrong. As far as he was concerned, nothing was wrong; he had done a good job. He *did* do a good job, if you forget about the ends and the values. I point out that professional science and professional philosophy are dedicated to the proposition of forgetting about the values, excluding them. This, therefore, must lead to Eichmanns, to atom bombs, and to who knows what (Maslow, 1971, p. 173)!"

Fromm (1964; 1971) has applied similar thoughts to the effects of technocratic values upon society:

"Briefly then, intellectualization, quantification, abstraction, bureaucratization, and reification—the very characteristics of modern industrial society, when applied to people rather than to things, are not the principles of life but those of mechanics. People living in such a system become indifferent to life and even attracted to death (1964, p. 59).

"Specifically, psychoanalysis will study the 'pathology of normalcy,' [if it is to be rejuvenated] the chronic low-grade schizophrenia which is generated in the cybernated, technological society of today and tomorrow (1971, p. 41)."

In spite of Skinner's (1971) "rational" justification—based upon the distortion of a single research paradigm—man has a choice. It is possible to select our values, and to expand our view of man by means of the methods we utilize for understanding him. Psychologists are not required to view man as a controlled, submissive automaton, or utilize techniques which promote, and therefore justify, this conception. It is time for the type of caution in psychology that Kass (1971) has provided for biomedical research;

> "We must all get used to the idea that biomedical technology makes possible many things we should never do (1971, p. 787)."

It may be true that reliance upon an environmentalistic conditioning model will result in the robot behavior that Skinner predicts, but it is certainly true that psychology does not need to *choose* this view of man as a foundation for methodological or theoretical decisions. Chein (1972, pp. 17-43) has provided an excellent example of the feasibility of a scientific approach based upon a view of man as an "active, responsible, free agent."

The primary problem for contemporary psychology, for contemporary society, is not irrationality and superstition, although they exist and can be disruptive; the issue is "rationality" severed from humanity. It is "rationality," untempered by feeling, experience, and value, which leads to the manipulation and degradation of people as the behavior modifiers "do a good job." It is "rationality," on the part of technocrats, in the name of fighting communism, that keeps us on the brink of atomic war, and it is "rationality" derived from the mindless pursuit of increased productivity which pushes us into unsolvable pollution. The present volume offers no panacea; it does, however, attempt to focus upon the role of value in the psychologist's quest for scientific respectability.

REFERENCES

Allport, G. W., "The General and the Unique in Psychological Science," in E. A. Southwell, & M. Merbaum (Eds.), *Personality: Readings in Theory and Research*. Belmont, California: Wadsworth, 1964.

Chein, I., *The Science of Behavior and the Image of Man*. New York: Basic Books, 1972.

Fromm, E., *The Heart of Man*. New York: Harper & Row, 1964.

Fromm, E., *The Crisis of Psychoanalysis*, Greenwich, Connecticut: Fawcett, 1971.

Giorgi, A., *Psychology as a Human Science: A Phenomenologically Based Approach.* New York: Harper & Row, 1970.

Heider, F., "On Perception and Event Structure and the Psychological Environment," *Psychological Issues*, 1959, 1, Monograph 3.

James, W., *The Philosophy of William James*, New York: Modern Library, 1953.

James, W., *Pragmatism*, New York: Meridian, 1955.

Kass, L. R., "The New Biology: What Price Relieving Man's Estate?" *Science*, 1971, 174, 779-788.

Klein, G. S., *Perception, Motives and Personality.* New York: Knopf, 1970.

Maslow, A. H., *The Farther Reaches of Human Nature.* New York: Viking, 1971.

Oppenheimer, R., "Analogy in Science," in F. T. Severin (Ed.), *Humanistic Viewpoints in Psychology.* New York: McGraw-Hill, 1965.

Skinner, B. F., *Beyond Freedom and Dignity.* New York: Knopf, 1971.

Von Bertalanffy, L., *Robots, Men, and Minds.* New York: Braziller, 1967.

BIBLIOGRAPHY

Allport, F. H., *Theories of Perception and the Concept of Structure.* New York: Wiley, 1955.

Allport, G. W., "The Emphasis on Molar Problems," in M. H. Marx (Ed.), *Psychological Theory.* New York: Macmillan, 1951.

Allport, G. W., "The General and the Unique in Psychological Science," in E. A. Southwell & M. Merbaum (Eds.), *Personality: Readings in Theory and Research.* Belmont, California: Wadsworth, 1964.

Barron, F., *Artists in the Making.* New York: Seminar Press, 1972.

Bergmann, G., "Sense and Nonsense in Operationalism," in F. T. Severin (Ed.), *Humanistic Viewpoints in Psychology.* New York: McGraw-Hill, 1965.

Bonner, H., "The Proactive Personality," in J. F. T. Bugental (Ed.), *Challenges of Humanistic Psychology.* New York: McGraw-Hill, 1967.

Breger, L., Hunter I., & Lane, R. W., "The Effect of Stress on Dreams," *Psychological Issues,* 1971, 7, Monograph 27.

Bridgman, P. W., "Remarks on the Present State of Operationalism," in F. T. Severin (Ed.), *Humanistic Viewpoints in Psychology.* New York: McGraw-Hill, 1965.

Bruner, J. S., *On Knowing: Essays for the Left Hand.* New York: Atheneum, 1965.

Buck, L. A., & Cuddy, J. M., "A Theory of Communication in Psychotherapy," *Psychotherapy: Theory, Research and Practice,* 1966, 3, 7-13.

Buck, L. A., & Kramer, A., "Opening New Worlds to the Deaf and the Disturbed," in J. J. Leedy (Ed.), *Poetry the Healer.* Philadelphia: Lippincott, 1973.

Buck, L. A., & Kramer, A., "Poetry as a Means of Group Facilitation," *Journal of Humanistic Psychology,* 1974, 14, 57-71.

Bugental, J. F. T., "Humanistic Psychology: A New Break-Through," *American Psychologist,* 1963, 18, 563-567.

Bugental, J. F. T., "The Challenge That Is Man," in J. F. T. Bugental (Ed.), *Challenges of Humanistic Psychology.* New York: McGraw-Hill, 1967.

Cantril, H. & Bumstead, C. H., "Science, Humanism, and Man," in F. T. Severin (Ed.), *Humanistic Viewpoints in Psychology.* New York: McGraw-Hill, 1965.

Carlson, R., "Where Is the Person in Personality Research?" *Psychological Bulletin,* 1971, 75, 203-219.

Cassirer, E., *An Essay on Man.* Garden City, New York: Doubleday, 1944.

Chein, I., *The Science of Behavior and the Image of Man.* New York: Basic Books, 1972.

Demos, R., "Psychoanalysis: Science and Philosophy," in S. Hook (Ed.), *Psychoanalysis: Scientific Method and Philosophy.* New York: Grove, 1960.

Dewey, J., *Intelligence in the Modern World.* New York, Modern Library, 1939.

Erikson, E. H., *Childhood and Society,* 2nd ed. New York: Norton, 1963.

Eysenck, H. J., "The Effects of Psychotherapy," in H. J. Eysenck (Ed.), *Handbook of Abnormal Psychology.* New York: Basic Books, 1961.

Freeman, T., Cameron, J. L., & McGhie, A., *Studies on Psychosis.* New York: International Universities Press, 1966.

Freud, S., *An Outline of Psychoanalysis.* New York: Norton, 1949.

Freud, S., *The Interpretation of Dreams.* New York: Basic Books, 1960.

Fromm, E., *The Art of Loving,* New York: Bantam, 1963.

Fromm, E., *The Heart of Man.* New York: Harper & Row, 1964.

Fromm, E., *Escape From Freedom.* New York: Avon, 1965.

Fromm, E., *The Sane Society.* New York: Fawcett, 1965.

Fromm, E., *The Crisis of Psychoanalysis.* Greenwich, Connecticut: Fawcett, 1971.

Giorgi, A., *Psychology as a Human Science: A Phenomenologically Based Approach.* New York: Harper & Row, 1970.

Haggard, E. A., & Isaacs, K. S., "Micromomentary Facial Expressions as Indicators of Ego Mechanisms in Psychotherapy," in L. A. Gottschalk, & A. H. Auerbach (Eds.), *Methods of Research in Psychotherapy*. New York: Appleton-Century-Crofts, 1966.

Hall, C. S., & Van de Castle, R. L., *The Content Analysis of Dreams*. New York: Appleton-Century-Crofts, 1966.

Hall, E. T., *The Hidden Dimension*. New York: Anchor, 1969.

Hartmann, H., "Psychoanalysis as a Scientific Theory," in S. Hook (Ed.), *Psychoanalysis: Scientific Method and Philosophy*. New York: Grove, 1960.

Hayakawa, S. I., "What Is Meant by Aristotelian Structure of Language," in S. I. Hayakawa (Ed.), *Language, Meaning and Maturity*. New York: Harper, 1954.

Heider, F., "On Perception and Event Structure, and the Psychological Environment," *Psychological Issues*, 1959, 1, Monograph 3.

Henry, J., *Pathways to Madness*. New York: Random House, 1971.

Hilgard, E. R., *Hypnotic Susceptibility*. New York: Harcourt, Brace & World, 1965.

Hilgard, J. R., *Personality and Hypnosis: A Study of Imaginative Involvement*. Chicago: University of Chicago Press, 1970.

Hook, S. (Ed.), *Psychoanalysis: Scientific Method and Philosophy*. New York: Grove, 1960.

Horowitz, L., "Theory Construction and Validation in Psychoanalysis," in M. H. Marx (Ed.), *Theories in Contemporary Psychology*. New York: Macmillan, 1963.

James, W., *The Principles of Psychology*, vol. I. New York: Dover, 1950.

James, W., *The Philosophy of William James*. New York: Modern Library, 1953.

James, W., *Pragmatism*. New York: Meridian, 1955.

Janis, I. L., *Psychological Stress*. New York: Wiley, 1958.

Janis, I. L., "The Psychoanalytic Interview as an Observational Method," in G. Lindzey (Ed.), *Assessment of Human Motives*. New York: Grove, 1960.

Jencks, C., & Riesman, D., *The Academic Revolution*. Garden City, New York: Doubleday, 1968.

Jourard, S. M., "Experimenter-Subject Dialogue: A Paradigm for a Humanistic Science of Psychology," in J. F. T. Bugental (Ed.), *Challenges of Humanistic Psychology*. New York: McGraw-Hill, 1967.

Jourard, S. M., *The Transparent Self*, revised ed. New York: Van Nostrand Reinhold, 1971.

Kass, L. R., "The New Biology: What Price Relieving Man's Estate?" *Science*, 1971, 74, 779-788.

Keniston, K., "Inburn: An American Ishmael," in R. W. White (Ed.), *The Study of Lives.* New York: Atherton, 1964.

Kilpatrick, F. P. (Ed.), *Explorations in Transactional Psychology.* New York: New York University, 1961.

King, J. A., "Ecological Psychology: An Approach to Motivation," in W. J. Arnold, & M. M. Page (Eds.), *Nebraska Symposium on Motivation.* Lincoln: University of Nebraska Press, 1970.

Klein, G. S., *Perception, Motives and Personality.* New York: Knopf, 1970.

Koch, S., "Psychological Science Versus the Science-Humanism Antinomy: Intimations of a Significant Science of Man," in J. A. Dyal (Ed.), *Readings in Psychology,* 2nd ed. New York: McGraw-Hill, 1967.

Koch, S., "Value Properties," in M. Grene (Ed.), "Toward a Unity of Knowledge," *Psychological Issues,* 1969, 6, Monograph 22.

Koffka, K., *Principles of Gestalt Psychology.* New York: Harcourt, Brace, 1935.

Kohler, W., *Gestalt Psychology.* New York: Liveright, 1947.

Korzybski, A., "The Role of Language in the Perceptual Processes," in R. R. Blake, & G. V. Ramsey (Eds.), *Perception: An Approach to Personality.* New York: Ronald, 1951.

Kris, E., "Psychoanalytic Propositions," in M. H. Marx (Ed.), *Psychological Theory.* New York: Macmillan, 1951.

Laing, R. D., *The Divided Self.* New York: Pantheon, 1969.

Langer, S. K., *Philosophical Sketches.* New York: Mentor, 1964.

Langer, S. K., *Mind: An Essay on Human Feeling,* vol. I. Baltimore: Johns Hopkins, 1967.

Lifton, R. J., *Death in Life.* New York: Random House, 1967.

Lindquist, E. F., *Design and Analysis of Experiments in Psychology and Education.* Boston: Houghton Mifflin, 1953.

Lipowski, Z. J., "Delirium, Clouding of Consciousness and Confusion," *Journal of Nervous and Mental Disease,* 1967, 145, 227-255.

Luborsky, L., "Momentary Forgetting During Psychotherapy and Psychoanalysis: A Theory and Research Method," in R. R. Holt (Ed.), *Motives and Thought: Psychoanalytic Essays in Honor of David Rapaport.* New York: International Universities Press, 1966.

McKellar, P., "The Method of Introspection," in J. Scher (Ed.), *Theories of the Mind.* New York: Free Press, 1962.

MacLeod, R. B., "The Phenomenological Approach to Social Psychology," in R. Tagiuri, & L. Petrullo (Eds.), *Person Perception and Interpersonal Behavior.* Stanford, California: Stanford University Press, 1958.

Maddi, S. R., "The Search for Meaning," in W. J. Arnold, & M. M. Page (Eds.), *Nebraska Symposium on Motivation.* Lincoln: University of Nebraska Press, 1970.

Mahl, G. F., "Gestures and Body Movements in Interviews," in J. M. Shlien (Ed.), *Research in Psychotherapy,* vol. III. Washington, D. C.: American Psychological Association, 1968.

Marx, M. H. (Ed.), *Psychological Theory.* New York: Macmillan, 1951.

Marx, M. H. (Ed.), *Theories in Contemporary Psychology.* New York: Macmillan, 1963.

Masling, J., "Role-Related Behavior of the Subject and Psychologist and Its Effects Upon Psychological Data," in D. Levine (Ed.), *Nebraska Symposium on Motivation.* Lincoln: University of Nebraska Press, 1966.

Maslow, A. H., "Deficiency Motivation and Growth Motivation," in M. R. Jones (Ed.), *Nebraska Symposium on Motivation.* Lincoln: University of Nebraska Press, 1955.

Maslow, A. H., "A Philosophy of Psychology: The Need for a Mature Science of Human Nature," in F. T. Severin (Ed.), *Humanistic Viewpoints in Psychology.* New York: McGraw-Hill, 1965.

Maslow, A. H., *Toward a Psychology of Being,* 2nd ed. New York: Van Nostrand Reinhold, 1968.

Maslow, A. H., *Religions, Values and Peak-Experiences.* New York: Viking, 1970.

Maslow, A. H., *The Farther Reaches of Human Nature.* New York: Viking, 1971.

Matson, F. W., "Humanization," in F. T. Severin (Ed.), *Humanistic Viewpoints in Psychology.* New York: McGraw-Hill, 1965.

May, R., "The Historical Meaning of Psychology as a Science and Profession," in J. A. Dyal (Ed.), *Readings in Psychology.* New York: McGraw-Hill, 1962.

May, R., "Scientific Presuppositions," in F. T. Severin (Ed.), *Humanistic Viewpoints in Psychology.* New York: McGraw-Hill, 1965.

Mogar, R. E., "Psychedelic (LSD) Research: A Critical Review of Methods and Results," in J. F. T. Bugental (Ed.), *Challenges of Humanistic Psychology.* New York: McGraw-Hill, 1967.

Moustakas, C., "Heuristic Research," in J. F. T. Bugental (Ed.), *Challenges of Humanistic Psychology.* New York: McGraw-Hill, 1967.

Murphy, G., "Psychological Views of Personality and Contributions to Its Study," in E. Norbeck, D. Price-Williams, & W. M. McCord (Eds.), *The Study of Personality.* New York: Holt, Rinehart & Winston, 1968.

Murphy, G. & Spohn, H. E., *Encounter With Reality*. Boston: Houghton Mifflin, 1968.

Oppenheimer, R., "Analogy in Science," in F. T. Severin (Ed.), *Humanistic Viewpoints in Psychology*. New York: McGraw-Hill, 1965.

Orne, M. T., "Hypnosis, Motivation, and the Ecological Validity of the Psychological Experiment," in W. J. Arnold, & M. M. Page (Eds.), *Nebraska Symposium on Motivation*. Lincoln: University of Nebraska Press, 1970.

Otto, H. A., "The Minerva Experience: Initial Report," in J. F. T. Bugental (Ed.), *Challenges of Humanistic Psychology*. New York: McGraw-Hill, 1967.

Piaget, J., & Inhelder, B., *The Psychology of the Child*. New York: Basic Books, 1969.

Polanyi, M., "The Creative Imagination," in M. Grene (Ed.), "Toward a Unity of Knowledge," *Psychological Issues*, 1969, 6, No. 2, Monograph 22.

Proshansky, H. M., Ittelson, W. H., & Rivlin, L. G., *Environmental Psychology: Man and His Physical Setting*. New York: Holt, Rinehart and Winston, 1970.

Rapaport, D., "Footnotes," in D. Rapaport (Ed.), *Organization and Pathology of Thought*. New York: Columbia University, 1951.

Rapaport, D., "Cognitive Structures," in H. E. Gruber, K. R. Hammond, & R. Jessor (Eds.), *Contemporary Approaches to Cognition*. Cambridge: Harvard University Press, 1957.

Rapaport, D., "The Structure of Psychoanalytic Theory," *Psychological Issues*, 1960, 2, Monograph 6.

Rapaport, D., *Emotions and Memory*. New York: Science Editions, 1961.

Rapaport, D., "States of Consciousness: A Psychopathological and Psychodynamic View," in *The Collected Papers of David Rapaport*. New York: Basic Books, 1967.

Rapaport, D., "The Scientific Methodology of Psychoanalysis," in *The Collected Papers of David Rapaport*. New York: Basic Books, 1967.

Rogers, C. R., "Persons or Science?" in F. T. Severin (Ed.), *Humanistic Viewpoints in Psychology*. New York: McGraw-Hill, 1965.

Rosenthal, R., "The Effect of the Experimenter on the Results of Psychological Research," in B. A. Maher (Ed.), *Progress in Experimental Personality Research*. New York: Academic Press, 1964.

Rosenthal, R., "Covert Communication in the Psychological Experiment," *Psychological Bulletin,* 1967, 67, 356-367.

Rosenthal, R., "Experimenter Expectancy and the Reassuring Nature of the Null Hypothesis Decision Procedure," *Psychological Bulletin,* 1968, 70, Monograph No. 6.

Rossi, A. M., "General Methodological Considerations," in J. P. Zubek (Ed.), *Sensory Deprivation: Fifteen Years of Research.* New York: Appleton-Century-Crofts, 1969.

Royce, J. R., "Psychology at the Crossroads Between the Sciences and the Humanities," in J. R. Royce (Ed.), *Psychology and the Symbol,* New York: Random House, 1965.

Royce, J. R., "Metaphoric Knowledge and Humanistic Psychology," in J. F. T. Bugental (Ed.), *Challenges of Humanistic Psychology.* New York: McGraw-Hill, 1967.

Ruesch, J., & Kees, W., *Nonverbal Communication.* Berkeley, California: University of California Press, 1959.

Sargent, S. S., "Humanistic Methodology in Personality and Social Psychology," in J. F. T. Bugental (Ed.), *Challenges of Humanistic Psychology.* New York: McGraw-Hill, 1967.

Seaborg, G. T., "Goals in Understanding Science," in R. V. Guthrie (Ed.), *Psychology in the World Today.* Reading, Massachusetts: Addison-Wesley, 1968.

Seeley, J. R., *The Americanization of the Unconscious.* New York: International Science Press, 1967.

Severin, F. T. (Ed.), *Humanistic Viewpoints in Psychology.* New York: McGraw-Hill, 1965.

Shapiro, S. B., "Myself as an Instrument," in J. F. T. Bugental (Ed.), *Challenges of Humanistic Psychology.* New York: McGraw-Hill, 1967.

Singer, J. L., *Daydreaming.* New York: Random, 1966.

Skinner, B. F., "Critique of Psychoanalytic Concepts and Theories," *Scientific Monthly,* 1954, 79, 300-305.

Skinner, B. F., *Walden Two.* New York: Macmillan, 1962.

Skinner, B. F., *Beyond Freedom and Dignity.* New York: Knopf, 1971.

Skinner, B. F., *About Behaviorism.* New York: Knopf, 1974.

Solley, C. M., & Murphy, G., *Development of the Perceptual World.* New York: Basic Books, 1960.

Spence, K. W., *Behavior Theory and Conditioning.* New Haven: Yale University Press, 1956.

Sperry, R. W., "An Objective Approach to Subjective Experience: Further Exploration of a Hypothesis," *Psychological Review,* 1970, 77, 585-590.

Szasz, T. S., *Ideology and Insanity.* Garden City, New York: Anchor, 1970.

Tart, C. T., *On Being Stoned: A Psychological Study of Marijuana Intoxication.* Palo Alto, California: Science and Behavior Books, 1971.

Tart, C. T., "States of Consciousness and State-Specific Sciences," *Science,* 1972, 176, 1203-1210.

Van Kaam, A. L., "Assumptions in Psychology," in F. T. Severin, (Ed.), *Humanistic Viewpoints in Psychology.* New York: McGraw-Hill, 1965.

Vernon, M. D., *The Psychology of Perception.* Baltimore: Penguin, 1962.

Von Bertalanffy, L., *Robots, Men and Minds.* New York: Braziller, 1967.

Wessman, A. E., & Ricks, D. F., *Mood and Personality.* New York: Holt, Rinehart & Winston, 1966.

White, R. W., "Sense of Interpersonal Competence," in R. W. White (Ed.), *The Study of Lives.* New York: Atherton, 1967.

Wilson, R. N., "Albert Camus: Personality, as Creative Struggle," in R. W. White (Ed.), *The Study of Lives.* New York: Atherton, 1964.

Wolman, B. B., & Nagel, E. (Eds.), *Scientific Psychology.* New York: Basic Books, 1965.

Zimbardo, P. G., "The Human Choice: Individuation, Reason, and Order Versus Deindividuation, Impulse, and Chaos," in W. J. Arnold, & D. Levine (Eds.), *Nebraska Symposium on Motivation.* Lincoln: University of Nebraska Press, 1969.

INDEX